SOWING THE SEEDS OF CHANGE

SOWING THE SEEDS OF CHANGE

THE STORY OF THE COMMUNITY FOOD BANK OF SOUTHERN ARIZONA

SETH SCHINDLER

SENTINEL PEAK

SENTINEL PEAK
An imprint of The University of Arizona Press
www.uapress.arizona.edu

We respectfully acknowledge the University of Arizona is on the land and territories of Indigenous peoples. Today, Arizona is home to twenty-two federally recognized tribes, with Tucson being home to the O'odham and the Yaqui. Committed to diversity and inclusion, the University strives to build sustainable relationships with sovereign Native Nations and Indigenous communities through education offerings, partnerships, and community service.

ISBN-13: 978-1-941451-10-6 (paperback)

Cover design by Carrie House, HouseDesign, LLC
Cover photos: Top left: Tucson Village Farm Stand at Santa Cruz River Farmers' Market (Kathleen Dreier Photography); Top right: Farmer with vegetables (mythja/Shutterstock); Bottom left: TEP Volunteers, 2018 Utility Bowl with Southwest Gas; Bottom right: Manzo Elementary School Children Harvesting Chard (Community Food Bank)
Designed and typeset by Leigh McDonald in Kepler 11/5 and Cassino WF (display)

Publication of this book is made possible in part by support from the Community Food Bank of Southern Arizona.

Unless otherwise noted, all photos are used with the permission of the Community Food Bank of Southern Arizona.

Library of Congress Cataloging-in-Publication Data
Names: Schindler, Seth, author.
Title: Sowing the seeds of change : the story of the Community Food Bank of Southern Arizona / Seth Schindler.
Description: Tucson : Sentinel Peak an imprint of University of Arizona Press, 2021. | Includes index.
Identifiers: LCCN 2021021552 | ISBN 9781941451106 (paperback)
Subjects: LCSH: Community Food Bank of Southern Arizona—History. | Food banks—Arizona—Tucson—History.
Classification: LCC HV696.F6 S35 2021 | DDC 363.8/8309791776—dc23
LC record available at https://lccn.loc.gov/2021021552

Printed in the United States of America
♾ This paper meets the requirements of ANSI/NISO Z39.48-1992 (Permanence of Paper).

Why a book about a food bank? Why one about the Community Food Bank of Southern Arizona? And why now?

While the Community Food Bank of Southern Arizona (CFB) is not just any food bank—it is, in fact, one of the oldest, most respected, and most innovative in America—this book's intent is not to laud its achievements. Rather, it is to help readers understand, and inspire them to believe, that the war against hunger, however difficult, is winnable. And not tomorrow. Now!

CONTENTS

FOREWORD

THE COMMUNITY FOOD BANK OF Southern Arizona (CFB) enjoys a reputation as one of the oldest, most respected, and most innovative food banks in the country. It was named "2018 Food Bank of the Year" by Feeding America, the national organization of food banks. It receives consistent high marks for fiscal management from Charity Navigator.

But mostly, the CFB is there when you need it—and many people do. More than 375 faith organizations and nonprofits rely on it to help feed congregants and clients. Families and individuals in five Arizona counties rely on it to supplement their budget with affordable fresh fruits and vegetables, as well as pantry staples.

In Tucson, the CFB is at the heart of our city's safety net. Walk into any one of its many locations and you'll find warm, friendly, caring people. Yet the CFB is a huge operation, with a $125-million budget and more than six-thousand volunteers.

Part of the CFB's reputation for innovation comes from looking at every aspect of food production and distribution and trying to come up with a program for each. The CFB helps with community and backyard gardens, even hosting its own community farm, Las Milpitas. It helps by collecting surplus food from supermarkets and produce from farms in Arizona and Mexico. It helps train formerly homeless, incarcerated, low-income, and unemployed people to work in food production. In its Caridad Community Kitchen's culinary training program, students learn everything it takes to work in a commercial kitchen, all while preparing delicious, nutritious meals for delivery to those who would otherwise go without.

This fine, profusely illustrated book tells the amazing story of the CFB and the dedicated people who have made it a model for other nonprofits to learn from, whatever their mission.

Jonathan Rothschild
Former Mayor of Tucson

SOWING THE SEEDS OF CHANGE

PART I

Feeding the Hungry of Southern Arizona

World Hunger, 2019 (World Food Programme)

CHAPTER 1

THE ROOTS OF THE COMMUNITY FOOD BANK OF SOUTHERN ARIZONA

I have the audacity to believe that people everywhere can have three meals a day for their bodies, education and culture for their minds, and dignity, equality and freedom for their spirits.

—MARTIN LUTHER KING, JR.

THE STORY OF THE COMMUNITY Food Bank of Southern Arizona (CFB) is the story of a unique community and its compassionate, sustained response to a local problem that is also a national and global one of staggering proportions. The United Nations World Food Programme estimates that, worldwide, about 800-million people suffer daily from food insecurity. Most live in the developing countries of Asia, Africa, and Latin America, where famine, extreme poverty, and malnutrition are commonplace. As you read this, millions in these countries are on the verge of starvation.

Even here in the United States, hunger is a major problem. According to the United States Department of Agriculture (USDA), in 2019 more than thirty-five million Americans lived in households defined as "food insecure." This means they often had to skip meals, eat less at meals, buy cheap, nonnutritious food, and/or feed their children but not themselves.

Contrary to stereotype, it's not just the homeless who are hungry. Many of the working poor, the disabled, senior citizens, single mothers, and even couples with two paychecks struggle daily to put food on the table for their families. Sadly, those suffering include the most vulnerable of all: thirteen million of our children.

The numbers in southern Arizona are no less shocking: 200,000 of its residents are food insecure.

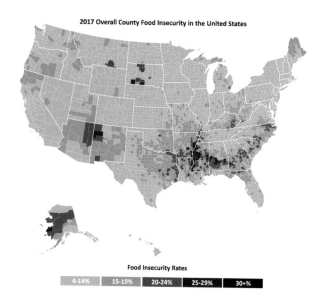

2017 Overall County Food Insecurity in the United States

Food Insecurity Rates

| 4-14% | 15-19% | 20-24% | 25-29% | 30+% |

Food Insecurity in the United States, 2017 (Feeding America)

2017 Overall County Food Insecurity in Arizona

Food Insecurity Rates

| 4-14% | 15-19% | 20-24% | 25-29% | 30+% |

Food Insecurity in Arizona, 2017 (Feeding America)

How can this be true in the richest country in the world, one with such an abundant food supply? The answer, unfortunately, is not simple, despite our sense that providing food for all Americans *should* be simple, and that most of us believe we have a moral obligation to help the less fortunate. This belief—a belief that, if not universal, has been shared and promoted by political and spiritual leaders here and around the world—is what makes us human.

Some might argue that this belief is even a defining feature of America's national character, bringing together people from across the political spectrum and of different means and religious beliefs. No one can deny that we have always been a charitable people, quick to share and to give of ourselves at our many soup kitchens and homeless shelters, for example. Is it any wonder, then, that America is recognized as the world leader in providing emergency disaster relief?

Clearly, solving the problem of hunger in America must begin by recognizing its existence. This also sounds simple, yet the extent of the problem was not fully recognized until the 1960s.

Although we had seen plenty of evidence of hunger during the Great Depression, perhaps we were distracted from addressing it by World War II and our subsequent efforts to help rebuild Europe, followed by the relative prosperity experienced here in the 1950s. Inspired by the success of President Franklin D. Roosevelt's New Deal programs in the 1930s, and depressed by what he saw when touring impoverished areas of the South, President John F. Kennedy initiated a pilot food voucher program. President Lyndon B. Johnson, also believing that poverty and hunger go hand in hand, made this pilot program permanent in 1964; it was a primary emphasis of his War on Poverty toward the goal of creating the Great Society.

CFB Food Distribution Line

Great Depression Bread Line (National Archives)

CFB Annual HungerWalk (David Sanders)

However admirable its goal, President Johnson's War on Poverty had mixed results, in part because of bureaucratic mismanagement of welfare programs. In addition, subsequent administrations, both Republican and Democratic, did not sustain the level of President Johnson's efforts. For a variety of reasons—including substantial cuts to the Food Stamp Program, now known as the Supplemental Nutrition Assistance Program, or SNAP—too many poor people still fell through the cracks, and the ranks of the food insecure continued to swell through both good and hard times.

If reliance on government alone isn't the answer, then what is? Some will say that individuals must assume responsibility for their own welfare. But the problem is so complex and enormous that all available sources of help are needed.

In the end, as the history of the CFB demonstrates, solving the problem of hunger requires all segments of a community to take responsibility and cooperate with each other. Who understands better than a community's members—our neighbors down the street and in our businesses, schools, local government, social service agencies, and places of worship—what works and what doesn't? A community cannot thrive unless all of us work as one for the common good. In a word, we must *share*. And, most importantly, we must share in helping eliminate hunger's root causes.

CHAPTER 2

HOPE SPROUTS IN THE DESERT

The war against hunger is truly mankind's war of liberation.
-PRESIDENT JOHN F. KENNEDY

WHEN YOU LOOK AT THE CFB today—the massive Punch Woods Multi-Service Center in Tucson, the many satellite branches and programs serving thousands across southern Arizona, and the hundreds of staff members and volunteers—it's hard to imagine it all began in a tiny, primitive warehouse.

This first headquarters might have been humble, but the dream behind it was as big and noble as it gets: to end hunger in Tucson. This was the vision of Mark Homan, Barry Corey, and Dan Duncan, founders of the CFB.

First CFB Building on South 4th Avenue, 1976 (*Arizona Daily Star*)

The CFB grew out of their work in the mid-1970s with a grassroots hunger advocacy group called the Food Action Coalition of Tucson. Duncan, Homan, and Corey recognized that the needs of the hungry weren't being met by the Food Stamp Program, which they saw as poorly managed. They were also alarmed by the amount of food going to waste in the city, and sensed that there had to be a way to make better use of it.

Inspired by the success of the St. Mary's Food Bank Alliance of Phoenix, the first food bank in the United States, these visionaries believed that the needs of the hungry would be met much more efficiently with a centralized mode of food distribution.

Punch Woods Multi-Service Center

Dan Duncan (left) and Mark Homan
(right) in First CFB Building, 1976
(*Arizona Daily Star*)

*We recognized that nonprofit agencies were spending
way too much time hustling emergency food for their
clients, rather than working on the long-term issues
with them so that they would not need emergency
food. Therefore, we started the food bank so that
with one thirty-second call an agency could order
a three-day supply of food for a family that they
could pick up later that day. Now the agencies could
spend the rest of their time helping their clients gain
employment, receive training, or deal with personal
and family issues.*

—DAN DUNCAN, CFB COFOUNDER
AND FORMER DIRECTOR

Dan Duncan, CFB Cofounder
and Former Director

Mark Homan, CFB
Cofounder and Founding
Board Member

Dan Duncan at Work, 1977
(*Arizona Daily Star*)

*Our original intention was to work to foster
conditions so that something like a food bank
would only be needed in case of real, short-term
emergencies. Our mantra was to 'put ourselves out of
business.' We would work for social change while at
the same time meet immediate needs.*

—MARK HOMAN, CFB COFOUNDER
AND FOUNDING BOARD MEMBER

Arnie Salverson, First CFB Volunteer (*Arizona Daily Star*)

First CFB Delivery Truck

Lew Murphy, Former Tucson Mayor and CFB Board Member

The CFB opened its doors in January 1976, with one employee, director Dan Duncan; one volunteer, Arnie Salverson; one delivery truck donated by Shamrock Farms; and a few boxes of donated food.

Mayor Lew Murphy of Tucson and Mayor Dan Eckstrom of South Tucson were enthusiastic early supporters. The City of Tucson, for example, donated what was left from the mayor's food drive, organized to aid striking miners the previous year. Included was seed money of $7,000. After leaving office, Mayor Murphy would continue to contribute significantly to the CFB's success as a long-term member of its board of directors.

The response from the community was astonishing: In the first year of operation alone, the CFB distributed 10,544 emergency food boxes and salvaged 80,000 pounds of food. It's doubtful that Dan Duncan and Arnie Salverson, much less the CFB's first board of directors, saw it coming. Nor could anyone have imagined the level of success they'd quickly achieve.

The emergency food boxes provided a three-day supply of the most basic food staples. Salvaged food—still edible but unsalable—came mostly from local supermarkets, wholesalers, and farms. One key to success at the very beginning might have been a purely practical one: making it as easy for individuals and commercial operators to donate the food as to throw it out. But equally decisive was how effectively the CFB promoted its mission by drawing the community's attention to the need and the importance of sharing, as captured so poignantly in its rallying cry, "Hunger *Does* Hurt."

The founders believed that the hunger-relief efforts could be improved substantially and carried out far more efficiently by having food distributed through Tucson's many nonprofits—welfare and faith-based agencies already serving the hungry. Clients would then remain connected to the agency they routinely visited for other services. This strategy proved so effective that, as the food banking movement later emerged in the early 1980s, the CFB's model was copied and became the standard used throughout the United States.

Today, the CFB also distributes food directly to clients, making it one of the few food banks in the country combining both modes. The founders, operating with severely limited resources and too busy just keeping up with the demand, probably never envisioned this strategic change. It was made operationally feasible only in 1996 with the 140,000 square feet of warehouse space provided by the Punch Woods Multi-Service Center.

By 1978, the CFB was distributing emergency food boxes through 120 local agencies. In 1980, about 23,000 boxes and 400,000 pounds of salvaged food were distributed. This amazing rate of growth would be the pattern in coming years.

The CFB's founders certainly discovered and implemented effective methods, but the organization's startling growth was also the result of factors outside their control—and not very positive ones. The founders also discovered that those in need were far more numerous than originally thought. The food bank's clients were not just the unemployed but, surprisingly, the *under*employed—the many working poor living primarily in Greater Tucson's traditionally economically depressed neighborhoods.

CFB's "Hunger *Does* Hurt" Rallying Cry

Although the founders may have initially underestimated the demand for the CFB's services, they had the vision to place its facilities in these neighborhoods, notably South Tucson, and establish an enduring bond with residents. The CFB would become a permanent community fixture, a neighbor that could be counted on to be there when times were especially tough.

Early Food Drive Sponsored by the University of Arizona (*Arizona Daily Star*)

Equally important was another discovery the founders made: that providing hunger relief in Tucson went far beyond the efforts of any one group. As best demonstrated by the success of the CFB's annual food drives (cosponsored by a variety of public and private organizations) and by the size and diversity of its volunteer work force, alleviating hunger would take the cooperative efforts of the whole community.

Tucson's religious community was quick to embrace the CFB's original mission and strategies; this was perhaps the single most important factor in the food bank's initial success. Despite their long-established role in helping the less fortunate, faith-based organizations took a big risk in partnering with an unproven group like the CFB. That their representatives—such as Reverend Kendall Baker of Tucson Metropolitan Ministries, Reverend Richard Bammeier of First Congregational Church, and Dr. Ben Brook, a leader of the Jewish community— were willing to serve and contribute as CFB board members testifies to what has long distinguished the CFB: the passion and energy of its staff, board, and volunteers, and their competence and resourcefulness in carrying out the organization's mission. These elements are the keys to the CFB's long-term success.

In addition to municipal and faith-based organizations, many other public and private segments of the Tucson community backed the CFB from the start. Local labor unions pitched in, as did several businesses. Tucson Electric Power and the United States Postal Service were two of the CFB's strongest early supporters and partners, and continue to be today, along with the University of Arizona, Tucson Parks and Recreation, and Tucson Unified School District.

This diverse network of community support provided an unusually strong foundation for growth, one that continues to pay dividends.

First Letter Carriers Food Drive, 1976 (*Arizona Daily Star*)

This is not to say that there were no opponents to the CFB, or that the organization didn't experience growing pains. Indeed, some charities, such as United Way, were slow to engage, and some prominent individuals in the city believed a food bank wasn't needed. They argued that existing charitable organizations, such as the Salvation Army, were doing a good enough job of helping the hungry.

There were also many times, early on, when the CFB seemed on the brink of collapse. Seasonal shortages of donated food, especially in summertime, were common, as were public pleas for help. Then there were times, during recessions in both the 1980s and 1990s, when it was necessary to cut the amount of food in the emergency boxes due to the increased demand, or to borrow money to buy food to fill the boxes.

These challenges underscore the fact that vision and good intentions alone can take an organization only so far; perseverance, resilience, and adaptability are also required. The CFB's founders and members of its early boards possessed these qualities, along with other equally necessary ones. The right mix of technical and management skills, coupled with the right personal chemistry, created not only a productive working atmosphere but a family-like one of mutual support and respect.

This isn't to suggest that there wasn't disagreement on matters both philosophical and strategic. In fact, as in other families, there was plenty of dissension. Yet, for the most part, any discord was balanced by a willingness to listen carefully to each other and to question constructively, to debate, test new ideas, and take reasonable risks.

Summer Emergency Food Shortage, 1976 (*Arizona Daily Star*)

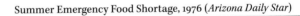

The founders wisely put together a board representing the opinions of a broad cross-section of the community. This mix, if volatile at times, sparked the kind of creative energy and innovative thinking that would distinguish the CFB in years to come. In the end, board members always managed to come together to ask the most important question: "How can we do it better?" More often than not, they had the right answers.

Without inspired leadership, few organizations succeed long term. In the case of the CFB, there's been no shortage of inspirational leaders through its storied forty-four-year history. However, at the CFB, leadership has always carried a distinctive flavor, one driven by the spirit of egalitarianism. The CFB leader most responsible for creating that spirit is Charles "Punch" Woods.

For a quarter century, from 1978 to 2003, Punch served as the CFB's executive director, guiding the organization through its most challenging phase of growth and providing the blueprint for its culture of caring, sharing, and innovating.

The early board was a wonderful mix of ragtag folks, some connected to faith communities, others who had connections with particular needed skills and community resources, and a few who had good connections with more influential community members. This brought together a valuable blend of talent, passion, and access.

The group was truly committed to the CFB's success, including its early mission of working for fundamental social change so as to ultimately eliminate the need for food banks. This meant that there was a willingness to engage in thoughtful strategic thinking and learning from each other, rather than posturing or any self-serving distractions. There was a clear and powerful spirit of mutual acceptance and intentional action.

—MARK HOMAN, CFB COFOUNDER AND FOUNDING CFB BOARD MEMBER

Founding Board Members

Rev. Kendall Baker, President	Michael Sandoval
Rev. Richard Bammeier	Carolyn Tufts
Mark Homan	Barbara Weymann
Barry Corey	Dr. Ben Brook
Jan Crawford	Tommy Thomas
Bill Diamond	Sam Lena
Howard Duncan	Isabel Garcia
Rene Gastelum	
Richard Kaffenberger	

Punch Woods, 1980, Former CFB Executive Director   (*Arizona Daily Star*)

In the beginning, the CFB's original mission was simply getting food to people through social service organizations that served the hungry.

When I was hired, with the inertia of almost two years in business as an all-volunteer organization, the CFB and the community were at a take-off point. This was done with food drives and fundraising, which quickly grew into also collecting edible unsalable foods from retail grocers and then wholesalers.

Later in my career, food banks like the CFB began organizing on a national level to solicit donations from food manufacturers and processors and to coordinate food banking nationwide.

—PUNCH WOODS, FORMER CFB EXECUTIVE DIRECTOR

CHAPTER 3

CULTIVATING A CULTURE OF CARING, SHARING, AND INNOVATING

There's enough on this planet for everyone's needs, but not for everyone's greed.
–MAHATMA GANDHI

PUNCH WOODS TELLS THE STORY of the epiphany he had while he was in college, studying abroad one winter in Veracruz, Mexico. At the waterfront, he watched corn being unloaded while local women gathered what had spilled onto the dock. This heartbreaking sight ignited what would become his life's work: helping those in need, first as a lay Methodist minister doing community development work in rural Mexico, then as the CFB's charismatic leader for a quarter century.

With Punch as its public face, is it any wonder that the CFB's mission was embraced so enthusiastically by Tucson's faith-based community? Secular organizations would quickly follow. How could they resist the message of this wise, humble, giving person?

Punch's engaging personality, passion for his work, resourcefulness, and respect for those he served are legendary, instilling hope and dignity in others. His can-do attitude, ever present no matter how insurmountable an obstacle seemed, was contagious, eliciting enthusiasm and loyalty in those he worked with. And when things seemed the darkest, his folksy humor and wisdom always brightened the world.

For many years in his popular column, "Punchline," featured in the CFB's *The More-Than-Occasional Newsletter*, Punch shared his vision of food banking with staff and the larger community.

Here in our hometown, many of our neighbors fear for their next meal. But they also feel guilty about not being able to provide for themselves. For many, this fear and guilt lead them to find food through the maze of welfare and social services. But many are too proud or embarrassed to say they need help.

Then there are those of us who have never been hungry. We deal with that same fear and guilt in different ways. Some deny there is hunger in Tucson, while others blame the poor for their own poverty. Many more donate and try to help in ways they know.

But our task is to eliminate the causes of hunger, and, therefore, remove the feelings of fear and guilt that drain the human spirit.

—PUNCH WOODS, "PUNCHLINE," JUNE 1982

Confronted by the problems of periodic shortages of food donations and downturns in the economy, including big cuts to the Food Stamp Program during the Reagan administration in the early 1980s, the CFB under Punch's leadership took steps to stabilize its operations and beef up capacity to meet the growing demand for its services.

In 1982, a new facility on West Twenty-Seventh Street was acquired, increasing warehouse capacity approximately thirty-fold, from about 600 to 18,000 square feet. By the end of the decade, this building, too, proved inadequate, and the CFB moved to one on South Park Avenue with nearly twice the space.

CFB's Second Building on West Twenty-Seventh Street, 1982

the
more - than - occasional
newsletter

**community
food bank, inc.**
Phone: 622-0525

VOL. XI, NO. 5
SEPTEMBER-OCTOBER 1990

CHARLES "PUNCH" WOODS, EXEC. DIR.
GRETCHEN TERMINI, EDITOR

—Photo By Molly ...re

PROJECT ISAIAH

The children pictured above are taking part in Project Isaiah, a Jewish community food drive to feed the hungry. This project is inspired by the Prophet Isaiah who said, "This is my chosen fast..share your bread with the hungry...do not turn away from people in need."

During their High Holy Days, September 19-28, food will be deposited at three locations: Congregation Anshei Israel, Temple Emanu-El, and the Tucson Jewish Community Center. A brown paper bag, provided by ABCO, will be included in the High Holiday edition of the Arizona Jewish Post. These will be used in the donations of non-perishable foods, such as: canned foods, soups, tuna, rice, peanut butter, beans, etc.

The Project Isaiah committee is co-chaired by Linda Tumarkin and Jim Lipsey. Placemats that will help educate on the hunger problem in Tucson, and coin envelopes and the brown bags are all being provided to inspire participation in this tremendous effort!

Working with Punch was the best part of my job. I could never have imagined having such a wonderful leader! He believed in me, guided me, gave me the instructions, and then let me do the work. He was always available for questions or to discuss any concerns I might have. His style of leading meetings and talking about how to serve those who need help was always so inspirational to me. His tone, demeanor, and style made working for and with him such a pleasure. His message has always been to care for, respect, and help others, and this permeated the organization at all levels, from the janitor to top management.

—JOY TUCKER, FORMER CFB STAFF MEMBER

Joy Tucker, Former CFB Staff Member

I began my career at the CFB in 1986, having just graduated with a master's in Latin American Studies and wanting to work in the nonprofit world with children and families in South America. But when I saw the posting in the Arizona Daily Star *for a job at the CFB, I jumped at the opportunity. They were hiring a Program Manager to start the Commodity Supplemental Food Program—CSFP [Food Plus]. Developing this program from scratch was one of the most exciting challenges in my long career. In March 1987, we opened our doors and began serving about 2,500 clients a month. By the end of that first year the number had almost doubled!*

Later in my career, I was given the opportunity to develop and oversee the creation of the branches in Nogales, Amado, and Marana; such programs as Kids Cafe and Caridad Community Kitchen; and, finally, the Willcox Distribution Center. In the process, I learned how to lead, to work as part of a team, to think out of the box, and, most importantly, to provide the best experience possible for our clients.

These opportunities and challenges are what made my work at the CFB so enjoyable and rewarding—the best career I could have ever asked for!

—JOY TUCKER, FORMER CFB STAFF MEMBER

The enslavement by poverty of the working poor is one of the worst things we can do to our fellow citizens, to the elderly, to the workers, and to their families. We should not, we cannot, depend on charity forever.

—PUNCH WOODS, "PUNCHLINE," MAY/JUNE 1990

While staff and volunteers were slowly added through the 1980s, the workforce remained fairly small. In 1983, for instance, there were only seven employees. One can only marvel at how they managed to meet the demand for the CFB's services. By the end of the decade, the CFB was distributing food boxes to about 80,000 clients.

In addition to finding the right strategies, Punch and the board were adept at finding the right people to make the CFB run smoothly: workers who were not only highly skilled, resourceful, and productive, but who shared a passion for helping the less fortunate and would stay the course through thick and thin.

Joy Tucker is a prime example. For thirty years, she contributed significantly to the CFB's success, as Punch's right-hand woman and in various supervisory roles such as Facilities Director. After Punch's retirement in 2003, Joy served as interim Executive Director.

Need and greed . . . How easily we confuse the two. How many fish do we need? How many anything do we need? When do we get to enough? Why is it so hard to know when a need is being fulfilled and not a greed?

—PUNCH WOODS, "PUNCHLINE," NOVEMBER 1989

FOOD PLUS BOXES

Food Plus Line

With the help of Congressman Jim Kolbe—an enthusiastic CFB supporter who'd later become a long-term board member—Punch worked tirelessly for several years to bring the federal Commodity Supplemental Food Program to Arizona, where it's known as Food Plus. In 1986, he finally succeeded. This achievement would shape the way the CFB operated for

years to come. More importantly, it would have an enormous impact on the lives of the people it served.

Food Plus provides qualifying mothers, children, and seniors with a monthly package of food. The introduction of Food Plus represented a revolutionary change at the CFB. For the first time, food was distributed directly to clients at the food bank's own facilities.

New fundraising tactics were employed in the 1980s to supplement the collection of food through annual food drives. In 1982, the CFB's first capital campaign was initiated, primarily to fund the acquisition and remodel of the much larger food storage and distribution facility on West 27th Street and the purchase of more trucks and fork lifts.

Client Picks Up Food Box, 1991 (*Arizona Daily Star*)

Paper Recycling Operation, 1977 (*Arizona Daily Star*, Lew Elliot)

Bruce McClelland, The Arizona Daily Star

Hunger riders — Bicycle riders take off in the Sixth Annual Hunger 100 Bike Ride to raise money for the Community Food Bank. The riders yesterday started from Green Fields Country Day School and afterward celebrated at the school with a picnic and an awards ceremony.

Sixth Annual Hunger 100 Bike Ride, 1989
(*Arizona Daily Star*, Bruce McClelland)

Emergency Food Bank 'A Fantastic Success'

By JUDY DONOVAN
Start Staff Writer

The Community Food Bank Inc., a city-wide system for distributing emergency food supplies, completed its first month of operation yesterday and Dan Duncan, executive director, calls it "a fantastic success."

stolen or lost and while they're awaiting replacement," Duncan said.

There will always be a need for emergency food in Tucson, he said, and the Food Bank is discovering new needy families every day.

But more than half of the $7,000 in food money on hand when the Food Bank opened

donate the food itself, to keep the program going," he said. "We've already had some food donated by bakeries and a dairy, and there may be more food vendors who can help."

Churches and organizations may take over food supplies on a rotating monthly basis. The

Newspaper Headline Announcing CFB's Success
(*Arizona Daily Star*)

Earlier, in the late 1970s, a newspaper recycling program was developed. Although this experimental side business brought in some needed cash, it was abandoned when the price of recycled paper dropped. Nevertheless, much was learned in the process that would be applied creatively to sustain the CFB's success.

More financially productive over the long term were the numerous promotional and fundraising special events developed that later were incorporated in the CFB's regular programming. Through the years, many Tucson residents have participated in these well-known hunger walks, bike-a-thons, summer "non-walks," quilt auctions, and benefit concerts.

Government and private-foundation grants, as well as large corporate and individual donations, were sought more systematically, with mostly positive results. In addition to stabilizing daily operations and making longer-term planning feasible, all these efforts brought the CFB's mission and activities more directly into the public eye locally, regionally, and nationally.

In a sense, the CFB was reinventing itself in response to the socioeconomic changes of those challenging times. Once again, it was ahead of the curve. Soon we would see the rise of the food bank movement in the United States.

Early Donation Check

CFB-Sponsored Mennonite Quilt Auction

Volunteers at West 27th Street Warehouse, 1991 (*Arizona Daily Star*)

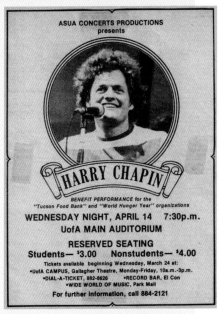

Harry Chapin Concert Fundraiser

Have you ever noticed that poor folks will share more easily than rich folks do?

— PUNCH WOODS, "PUNCHLINE," OCTOBER 1988

Matt Knott, Former President of Feeding America

The role of Second Harvest [now Feeding America] in its earliest days was to help expand the food banking model to new communities throughout the country, and to do so with a set of standards that would ensure good stewardship of food and funds so that donors and partners could support their local food bank with confidence.

Second Harvest's role was especially important at that time due to the growth of the food banking movement. From 1979 to 1989, for example, the number of food banks in the United States increased from 29 to 185.

— MATT KNOTT,
FORMER PRESIDENT OF
FEEDING AMERICA

In 1983, the CFB joined Second Harvest, the national network of food banks that is now called Feeding America. Through the sharing of ideas and techniques, this partnership improved the CFB's reach and the efficiency of its food acquisition, storage, and distribution operations.

Similar improvements were achieved when the CFB joined the Association of Arizona Food Banks (AAFB; now the Arizona Food Bank Network), also established in 1983. Its first and long-time director, Ginny Hildebrand, was instrumental in fostering cooperation among Arizona's early food banks, and in obtaining state and federal funding for their operations, by presenting their case to legislators in a unified voice: enthusiastic, well-informed, and persuasive.

With Ginny's help, and with Punch's as a Second Harvest board member, Arizona soon became a leader in the emerging food bank movement, drawing national attention to, and funding for, the needs of its less fortunate citizens. Even back then, the CFB and the community it served were widely recognized as special.

These organizational efforts at the state and federal levels also helped bring into focus the plight of the rural poor living *outside* Arizona's two major cities, Phoenix and Tucson. In the 1980s, to get help to these people of southern Arizona directly and regularly, the CFB opened small satellite branches in Ajo, Three Points, Green Valley, Amado, and Marana.

While tentatively made, this strategic decision to widen the organization's geographical reach set the stage for the later expansion of the CFB throughout southern Arizona, creating one of the largest centralized regional networks of food banks in the United States.

Ginny Hildebrand, Former Director of
the Association of Arizona Food Banks

My food banking career with the Association of Arizona Food Banks (AAFB) [now Arizona Food Bank Network] extended from 1983 to 2013. At first, the six-month-old organization, of which the CFB was a founding member, concentrated on coordinating food bank work and feeding more hungry people. But as the number of people in poverty grew, so did AAFB's mission.

To remain relevant to the need, the mission added identifying new food sources, acquiring refrigerated transportation equipment and/or services, and advocating for policy changes at the state and federal levels.

Success in the public policy/advocacy arena was key. Progress was first achieved in 1986 with the Arizona Legislature's approval of the Coordinated Hunger Line Item, budgeted then at $60,000. By 2013, this figure had increased dramatically to $1.7 million. By using an innovative process to blend state and federal funds channeled through the Arizona Department of Economic Security, Arizona's food banks coordinated efforts to handle and distribute, annually, millions of pounds of commodity and locally sourced foods.

By 2013, when I retired, AAFB had lobbied successfully for twenty bills and appropriations and, with Feeding America's help, numerous major federal food and nutrition initiatives.

—GINNY HILDEBRAND,
FORMER DIRECTOR OF
THE ASSOCIATION OF
ARIZONA FOOD BANKS

Amado CFB Branch

Tucson is unique in that its citizens care for each other. Unlike Phoenix, it always had a small-town feel, a single, naturally unified community that made food banking work more easily and effectively.

The CFB became distinctive in my mind the very first time I visited their food bank in the summer of 1985. Their staff was truly a team, focused on providing the best service possible to hungry people. They always looked for the opportunity to serve and bring the concept of 'freedom from hunger' to reality even before it was a term used across the country in the late 1990s.

Punch Woods' leadership was key, as he embodied the philosophy that 'I can always change a "no" into a "yes"; just give me time.'

—GINNY HILDEBRAND, FORMER DiRECTOR OF THE ASSOCIATION OF ARIZONA FOOD BANKS

Poverty is like the weather; everyone talks about it but nobody does anything. Just because the rain falls on both the good and the bad, it doesn't mean we can go on believing the poor will always be with us.

—PUNCH WOODS, "PUNCHLINE," JUNE 1990

CHAPTER 4

A TREE GROWS IN SOUTHERN ARIZONA

Volunteers have always been the strongest link of our food bank. This is the true 'community' part of our name. It takes all of us to care for one another.

–PUNCH WOODS

VOLUNTEERS ARE THE HEART AND soul of most service-oriented nonprofits, and the CFB is no exception. Yet, whether strategizing in the boardroom, working in a warehouse, or organizing a food drive, its volunteers are truly outstanding. If there is a single feature most indicative of the CFB's culture of caring and sharing, it is the vital contribution made by its volunteers—their passion and devotion and the consistently high quality of their work.

One measure of this is the volunteers' loyalty over long periods. Consider the CFB's many long-serving board members and their record of excellent service: Mark Homan (1975–1995), Barry Corey (1975–2008), Bill Young (1983–2008), Mark Fay (2003–2007), Jim Kolbe (1983–2008), and Betsy Bolding (1991–2008).

Betsy Bolding, Former CFB Board Member

The early CFB boards were quite 'hands on,' with opportunities to get to know each other and to learn about our programs. On one such day, the board and some staff headed to the Sonoita area for salvaging fresh fruit, aka gleaning. We all got set up—ladders, baskets, picker poles, etc.—raring to start picking peaches . . . I think it was. But we barely got started when a huge rainstorm hit and we spent most of the day crowded in the small house on the owner's property, waiting for the rain to stop! Bonding: 10, Gleaning: 0.

Service on the CFB board was extremely gratifying, meaningful, and fun, as well. In a way, the 'education' those years provided me was life-changing, as it significantly informed my future work with vulnerable families both professionally and as a volunteer.

—BETSY BOLDING, FORMER CFB BOARD MEMBER

Bill Young, Former CFB Board Member

Community is and has been what makes the CFB work. Board members have been diverse and strong advocates for the needs of the community. They have been involved and strong advocates for community member clients. They have been aware of the incredible generosity of the community and dedicated to using the community gifts effectively and efficiently. The staff have been passionately focused on the mission. They have been innovative and have effectively led the organization with a view of the long-term as well as immediate needs.

I had a background and interest in hunger issues and in the production, processing, and distribution of food and agricultural products. I believe strongly that community is vital and was impressed by the community involvement at the CFB. I felt that my background was unique and would be useful in advocating both for the donor and the recipient members of the parts of the community.

— BILL YOUNG, FORMER CFB BOARD MEMBER

Barry Corey, Cofounder and Former CFB Board Member

Jim Kolbe, Former CFB Board Member

Mark Fay, Former CFB Board Member

34

Among these notable, loyal board members is Terri Valenzuela, a client who, beginning in the mid-1990s, served for many years with distinction and who illustrates the CFB's commitment to egalitarianism. After her death, her son Andres came aboard; he continues to serve today.

Terri Valenzuela, Former
CFB Board Member

Andres Valenzuela,
CFB Board Member

My mom, Terri, was a single mother with severe rheumatoid arthritis and was unable to work. We didn't have enough money for housing, let alone food, so my mom turned to the CFB for help. As a kid, I remember going to the CFB's pantry and picking up our food boxes.

While I was in elementary school, she looked for a way to give back and started to get invited to speak to groups on behalf of the CFB, to share her story about how much impact the CFB had on us and many others in the community. She was able to give a voice and face to the clients of the CFB.

I remember how proud my mom was when she was asked to be the first client to serve on the CFB's board. I think that she, beyond being a mother, was most proud of this achievement. Her disability made even attending board meetings incredibly challenging. Her dedication inspired me, and I knew that when I was older, I wanted to do something to make her just as proud.

Unfortunately, I didn't realize my opportunity would come only after she passed away. With Punch Woods' help, I was accepted to fill her position on the board, and to this day it's my greatest accomplishment in life. Not only am I representing her legacy, I am giving back to an organization that allowed me to grow up and succeed, without having to go hungry. I owe most of my success in school and in my professional life to the CFB.

—ANDRES VALENZUELA,
CFB BOARD MEMBER

Long-term loyalty also characterizes the CFB's generous benefactors. Several of the early, major donors continue to contribute substantially today: local companies like Tucson Electric Power, Fry's Food Stores, and Southwest Gas; foundations like Tucson Foundations; and such individuals as Jim and Sandy Peebles, Lisa and Gary Israel, and Jim Click.

Jim Click, CFB Donor

The CFB plays such an important role in Tucson by providing food for the less fortunate. Years ago, the CFB was short on staples for the holidays. At that moment, I decided to do a matching grant. A good friend of mine matched my grant almost immediately! Ever since that day, we have continued this tradition every year. Giving back to your community is the best investment you can ever make.

—JIM CLICK, CFB DONOR

Among today's hundreds of CFB agency partners are quite a few that were there at the very beginning, providing essential support: the many neighborhood centers administered by Tucson Parks and Recreation; the Salvation Army; Tucson Metropolitan Ministries; and several churches, such as First Congregational, United Methodist, and Trinity Presbyterian.

However, it is the largely unknown volunteers working daily who deserve special mention. From its early days, the CFB has been blessed to have the services of these unsung heroes, such as the Mennonite Volunteers, Presbyterian Church Young Adult Volunteers, AmeriCorp Volunteers, Peace Corps Fellows, and Emerson Hunger Fellows. They have been joined by tens of thousands of local residents who give selflessly for the common good. The majority of these are Tucson's many retired senior citizens.

One can't help but wonder if having such a large pool of retirees to draw upon has contributed to the CFB's unusual level of success, giving it a distinct advantage over food banks in most other states. Perhaps it has. Yet equally important in attracting and keeping so many volunteers of all stripes is what the food bank offers them: a friendly, family-like work environment where respect for others is the name of the game.

Many say their work at the CFB is the most rewarding they've ever done, no doubt because the results are so obvious, especially in the smiles of those they help. It doesn't hurt, either, that their work is done in well-run programs, which makes being productive so easy and enjoyable.

Some volunteers, such as Virginia Wyly and Keith Hutton, served for decades, and many staff members began as volunteers, including Audra Christophel, originally a Mennonite Volunteer.

TEP Volunteers, 2018 Utility Bowl with Southwest Gas

CFB Volunteers, 1995 (*Arizona Daily Star*)

CFB Volunteers, 2008

For the past sixteen years I have done volunteer work at the CFB, and over the past twelve for one of its agencies, the Cross Streets Community at Southside Presbyterian Church, where I help procure and prepare food from the CFB.

In the warehouse of the Agency Market I also assist new agency shoppers, as well as clean the area and do whatever is necessary to keep it running smoothly.

It is simple work, yet educational and very rewarding. I learn about how different groups contribute to our community, and see on a daily basis the positive impact the CFB has on their work and the people they serve. In my work at Southside, I find it especially gratifying to see clients gain the confidence to seek job training or find jobs.

— VIRGINIA WYLY, CFB VOLUNTEER

Keith Hutton, CFB Volunteer

I've been volunteering with the food bank since 1988. I've worked, for example, in the warehouse checking cans for damage, and rode the bread truck for quite a while, collecting day-old bread.

It's very satisfying to work here, to know we're helping people. And so many good people work here, too. I encourage others to get involved, tell them about my experience, and ask them to give it a try.

— KEITH HUTTON,
CFB VOLUNTEER

Virginia Wyly, CFB Volunteer

The CFB has grown and flourished with the community. We are pleased to have so many of our foundation donors realize the need to feed the hungry and allow us to continue their support of the CFB long after they have gone.

— LINDA LOHSE,
MANAGING DIRECTOR,
TUCSON FOUNDATIONS

I came to the CFB as a Mennonite Volunteer in 2009 to run the consignment program, which is now called the Abundant Harvest Cooperative. I worked with backyard gardeners to aggregate and sell produce at a shared table at its farmers markets. Both sides of my family have been farming for generations, and I have a deep connection to land, food, and community. As a young and excited volunteer, I was thrilled to have the opportunity to work with and learn from others focused on the intersections of social justice, food access, and systems change.

After one year I was hired on as staff. One year turned into two years, and two turned into nine! My role has shifted over time, but I stay with the CFB because I continue to be challenged in my work—to learn and grow personally and professionally, and to deepen my skills as a practitioner of justice-based community work. I stay with the CFB because at our best we continue to adapt over time; to value and foreground relationships; and to grapple with tough questions that challenge our collective thinking, our role, and the way we listen, engage, and respond to our community.

—AUDRA CHRISTOPHEL, CFB STAFF MEMBER

Audra Christophel, CFB Staff Member

Elsa Pratt, CFB Staff Member

On April 25, 1983, I began working at the CFB, and I'm still here 36 years later! This is not only because I've enjoyed my different jobs, such as Bookkeeper, Grants Administrator, and Sourcing Operations Coordinator, but because I've always believed in the CFB's mission and its services to the people of Tucson.

It all started with Punch's vision. Yet we wouldn't be where we are today without community support and a lot of good people working hard together.

—ELSA PRATT, CFB STAFF MEMBER

Perhaps it's not surprising, then, that this pattern of long-term loyalty extends to staff. With his quarter century of service, Punch set a good example and, indeed, a very high bar. However, several of his coworkers, such as Joy Tucker (1986–2017), Elsa Pratt (1983–present), and Jean Fox (1989–2015) have given Punch a run for his money.

This pattern appears alive and well among a new generation of CFB staff, including Sandie Hinijos (2001–present), Kristen Quinnan (2003–2019), Jacob Coldsmith (2006–present) and George Fahrman (2002–present). Although the reasons for their long service may differ, it's clear that many employees continue to find their work highly gratifying.

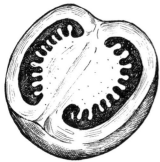

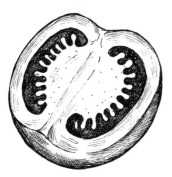

George Fahrman, CFB Staff Member

I have been working for 18 years at the CFB. In my job as Transportation Coordinator, I make sure all of the vehicles work right and are DOT [Arizona Department of Transportation] inspected.

During my job interview years ago, I was asked if I had 'empathy for the poor.' My response was, I am poor! Now I'm not. Thanks to my job at the CFB, I now own my house and have a 401k retirement plan. So, the 'shorten the line' program here worked for me and someday I'll be able to retire and volunteer at the CFB, and help others like myself. Due to the CFB, I will complete my goals in life.

—GEORGE FAHRMAN,
CFB STAFF MEMBER

Jacob Coldsmith, CFB Staff Member

I've worked at the CFB since 2006, and now help supervise our fleet operations. I started in what was then called Tucson's Table and is now called Agency Market. Food rescue and the multiplying effect of agency relationships were what originally attracted me to the CFB. Making sure that good food goes to good use is such a common-sense solution to hunger and food waste.

What has kept me engaged with the work at the CFB is that it continually pushes me to grow and be better. Sometimes that means being a better logistician. Sometimes it means being a better manager and/or leader. Often it means being a better individual. So far, I have never stopped learning through my work at the CFB.

—JACOB COLDSMITH,
CFB STAFF MEMBER

If the staff, like the volunteers, have found their work so rewarding, then the CFB must have been doing something right in its first quarter century. But, more importantly, what about those it served in the early days? Were they satisfied, too?

Although client-satisfaction surveys and scientific assessments of the effectiveness of the CFB's programs would not be conducted until several years later, an answer to this vital question can be gleaned from comments of today's clients who have contributed to the CFB's recent *Voices* series of publications. These poignant stories suggest that the CFB has long made a positive impact on the lives of those it serves.

Glen, CFB Client

For twenty-eight years I had my own company and was doing well. Then, suddenly, due to a disabling illness, I couldn't work anymore. I lost it all, and ended up on the street.

Thank God, I've been able to pick myself up. I'm so thankful to the people at the food bank, because without their help I would have starved.

—GLEN, CFB CLIENT

We try to give our children healthy food, but it's not the same as in Mexico. Here the food isn't as fresh.

We're changing that in the garden at our kids' school, Ochoa Elementary. With the help of the food bank, we are growing vegetables and making salads for our kids.

First they're skeptical and say, 'What's this?' But they eat it. Sometimes they come home and even say, 'Mom, look what I ate today!'

—MARBELLA, CFB CLIENT

Marbella and Family, CFB Clients

Debbie, CFB Client

I don't think my mother realized how broke I really was. But when I went through that situation, she told me to check out the food bank. That's when I realized I don't have to go to bed hungry.

I've also been volunteering at the food bank for seven years now. And if I hear that someone's having trouble putting food on the table, I tell them about the food bank. They help in any way they can, and there's more than just food. For instance, I used the Giffords Center [Gabrielle Giffords Resource Center] there when I had to renew my food stamps.

People say, 'The food bank?' And I say, 'Yes, they do so much!'

—DEBBIE, CFB CLIENT

Kesha, CFB Client

I had to send my son to school without food, and it broke my heart. It was tough to come to the food bank the first time. My biggest fear was that I'd run into someone I knew, and have to explain why I was there.

But when you allow someone else to help you with something as basic as food, you can't be the same afterwards—not feel love. It was life-altering, coming to the food bank.

—KESHA, CFB CLIENT

I first came to Tucson some twenty years ago. I came alone and have no family here. I was staying at the Salvation Army shelter and I overheard someone talking about the food bank. I went there and got not just food but help getting food stamps.

I'd applied for food stamps several times before, but each time was denied. The people at the food bank helped me fill out the application properly, and I finally got approved.

Now I'm not hungry all the time.

—FRANCISCO, CFB CLIENT

Francisco, CFB Client

CHAPTER 5

HARVESTING THE FRUITS OF INNOVATION

The test of our progress is not whether we add more to the abundance of those who have much; it is whether we provide for those who have little.

–PRESIDENT FRANKLIN D. ROOSEVELT

THE NUMBERS SEEM TO INDICATE that, in its first quarter century, the CFB was satisfying the needs of the hungry. By the mid-1990s, the CFB was distributing millions of pounds of food annually, providing more than 25,000 meals per day.

But research data would soon prove what staff at the CFB's Hunger Awareness Resource Center had long suspected: a hidden hunger gap still existed. Punch, along with his staff and board, needed to find creative solutions to help those identified as not yet adequately served: infants, children, and seniors. While the first experimental steps to help low-income seniors were taken in 1980, when the We-Care-A-Van program was initiated to serve the homebound, it wasn't until the mid- to late-1990s that efforts to close the hunger gap had sustained success.

CFB Staff, 1996

In 1996, the Infant Food Box and Senior Brown Bag programs were introduced.

The infant program provides a ten-day supply of formula; if they wish, qualifying mothers also receive referrals to other family services available at the CFB or elsewhere. Many seniors on limited fixed incomes often need a bit of help getting by and, if a social service agency makes the request, the CFB provides them with a monthly bag of food.

To address the special needs of the young, a pilot project called the Kids Cafe Program was launched in 1998 at the Boys & Girls Club on Thirty-Sixth Street. Hot meals and snacks are provided after school to children between five and eighteen years old. Equally important, kids also participate in nutrition education activities. The model proved highly successful, and, over the next few years, it was expanded to other sites at several neighborhood centers and agencies. Eventually, it would become one of the CFB's signature community outreach programs.

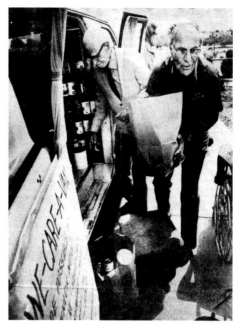
We-Care-A-Van, 1980 (*Arizona Daily Star*)

The decision to include these nutrition education activities was a turning point in the evolution of the CFB. It was one of its first forays into what would later become a major priority: moving beyond hunger relief by empowering the poor through food education. A few years later, in recognition of the fact that the Kids Cafe Program didn't completely meet the needs of some children, the complementary Snak

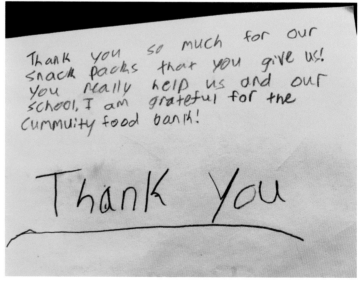
Note from Child at Kids Cafe

Citrus Gleaning (*left*), Vegetable Gleaning (*right*)

Pak Program (now the BackPack Program) was introduced with the financial assistance of Tucson Electric Power. At schools and other sites in their neighborhoods, children are given food to take home for the weekend.

This program proved highly successful and would grow substantially. In 2018, more than 62,000 BackPacks of food went home with local kids in need.

Thinking outside the food box to help more of the needy and reaching out to engage new segments of the community in this work would become the CFB's main strategies over the course of the 1990s. During this decade, the Gleaning Program was also developed.

Despite still being edible, crops are often left in fields or orchards for a variety of reasons. The CFB gained the cooperation of local farmers who otherwise would have let this produce go to waste. Jean Fox, the first and long-term coordinator of the Gleaning Program, was instrumental in making all this work. Volunteers gather citrus fruit, apples, and various kinds of vegetables, which are then distributed in food boxes to participating agencies or directly to clients.

Although the scale of the Gleaning Program would later be reduced as more reliable and substantial sources of fresh produce became available, the general concept of eating healthier food would become a priority of today's CFB.

Jean Fox, Former CFB Staff Member

I worked for ten years, 1989 to 1999, managing the Gleaning Program and its mainly volunteer workforce, then another fifteen running the Agency Relations division. For over twenty-five years I helped the CFB grow and meet the needs of our clients, and this gave me great satisfaction. But to be honest, when I first started, my work was just a nine-to-five job to me. It was only later that I learned how important this work was for our community. Helping the less fortunate became my calling, what I wanted to do with the rest of my life.

The CFB back then was like a big family, which made it a comfortable place to work. Everyone, including volunteers and clients, was treated with respect. What always impressed me was the passion for their work that my fellow workers all shared. This was contagious, what made the CFB function so well, despite all the obstacles we continually faced. The other thing that distinguished the CFB was the good communication among the staff, beginning at the top, and the rapport we had with the board. I doubt I could've found a better place to work.

—JEAN FOX, FORMER CFB
STAFF MEMBER

As Agency Relations Manager of Tucson's Table, Jean Fox oversaw the various operations entailed in organizing donated, gleaned, and salvaged food and distributing it to the CFB's agency partners. First developed with a generous grant from the United Parcel Service Foundation, Tucson's Table—now called Agency Market—would grow rapidly and evolve into a major component of the CFB we know today.

Tucson's Table

Holiday Share (*Arizona Daily Star*)

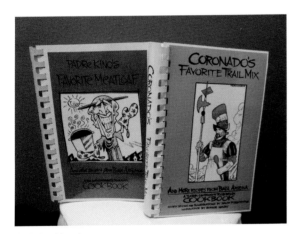

CFB Cookbooks

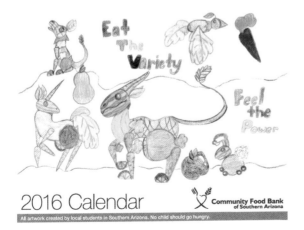

Kids' Calendar, 2016

Through the 1990s, the CFB continued to discover and develop creative ways to promote its mission and share with the community. It initiated and helped organize or sponsor various culinary festivals and such popular annual community events as the Holiday Share, along with the CARE Fair, which provided food, school supplies, immunizations, and other social services to low-income families.

In the mid-1990s, the CFB partnered with Habitat for Humanity, stocking the pantries of newly built homes for low-income Tucsonans. The CFB also produced two engaging cookbooks: *Padre Kino's Favorite Meatloaf* and *Coronado's Favorite Trail Mix*—as well as the still-popular annual Kids' Calendar, featuring drawings and quotes by children.

In recognition of its sustained and innovative efforts to help the hungry, the CFB received the Victory Against Hunger Award from the Congressional Hunger Center in 1998. Other awards would follow, as the CFB's reputation grew as a national leader in the food bank movement.

The Value Foods grocery store was another innovative project introduced in the mid-1990s. Designed to supplement the Food Plus program, this brick-and-mortar store sold prepackaged food and meals to the public at wholesale prices. Food stamps were accepted for payment. Although this nonprofit grocery store was later phased out, it demonstrates another distinctive feature of the CFB's culture: a willingness to experiment and take risks.

Perhaps the greatest risk ever taken by the CFB was the decision in 1996 to purchase the giant Levy's department store warehouse at 3003 South Country Club Road. This decision was hotly debated by the board at the time, and it was far from unanimous. There was even opposition from the larger Tucson community. Editorial writers in local newspapers questioned the wisdom of the move, claiming the CFB was overextending itself.

Nevertheless, Punch pushed hard to go ahead. Dreaming the impossible dream? How could they possibly pull it off financially, or make such an enormous space work operationally? After all, their then-current income would barely support such a debt. And their operations would fill only a portion of the available space.

Value Foods Grocery Store

Punch Woods Multi-Service Center

Warehouse at Multi-Service Center

Truck Fleet at Multi-Service Center

At the time of the purchase of the Levy's warehouse, the real estate sector of the economy had been devastated and excessive debt was a major factor in that. There was a concern that taking on the debt and administrative requirements of such a large building was not prudent. Fortunately, the staff were strong and effective advocates for the purchase, and the majority of the board felt that the leverage of the purchase would allow for much more effective operations and provide a better service to our clients.

—BILL YOUNG, FORMER CFB BOARD MEMBER

The board spent many meetings wrestling with the decision to buy the behemoth Levy's warehouse, but in the long run, Punch, who operated on confidence and hope, won over our risk-averse group. The whole thing scared me to death: taking on such debt and a huge albatross of a building that we couldn't imagine filling by renting space to other nonprofits, let alone ever using it entirely ourselves. Not in our wildest dreams did we think food demands and increasing family needs would grow to require every square foot of that enormous space!

—BETSY BOLDING, FORMER CFB BOARD MEMBER

Punch, as usual, was thinking far ahead, but he wasn't just dreaming. He was seeing the handwriting on the wall: the likely spike in the demand for the CFB's services, with further cuts to the Food Stamp Program looming in the wake of the Clinton administration's 1996 plan to "end welfare as we know it."

In the mid-1990s, the CFB also faced a new problem: Salvaged food was harder and harder to obtain, as manufacturers, distributors, and retailers were becoming increasingly efficient. Finding other, more reliable food sources would prove challenging. But these early efforts would be rewarded some two decades later with the development of the CFB's highly successful Produce Rescue Program, which today salvages and distributes hundreds of thousands of tons to its pantries and partners throughout the region.

In acquiring the new building, Punch and the board also saw the opportunity to achieve two new strategic goals: first, to expand their reach in other directions by partnering with nonprofits providing different, yet compatible, social services; and, second, to use this larger facility to develop programs previously impractical at the old sites. The new headquarters would thus truly become a *multi-service* facility as its current name indicates: The Punch Woods Multi-Service Center.

The first goal was achieved quickly by leasing surplus office space in the new building to compatible human service organizations such as Mobile Meals of Southern Arizona, Southern Arizona Legal Aid, Arizona Lions Vision Center, and the Arizona Special Supplemental Nutrition Program for Women, Infants, and Children (WIC). At the same time, the lease income put the CFB back on its feet financially by helping to offset its much larger mortgage payments.

The Multi-Service Center's location and design would later present practical problems for these nonprofits, and several would leave. However, the guiding principle of this "one-stop shop" would bear fruit as the CFB grew to the point that it alone could conveniently provide many of these social services to its clients. Ultimately, the risk taken in acquiring the property was richly rewarded.

The second and more ambitious goal of developing new programs aimed at empowering the poor would take more time to realize, but would be far more consequential in the CFB's eventual transformation from a hunger-relief organization to one emphasizing hunger and poverty prevention.

CHAPTER 6

SOWING THE SEEDS OF FOOD JUSTICE

Hunger is not a problem. It is an obscenity.

–ANNE FRANK

FROM THE VERY BEGINNING, THE CFB's founders understood that their efforts to provide hunger relief were but a Band-Aid solution to the deep-seated problem of poverty in America. The CFB's mission statements throughout the last quarter of the twentieth century—echoed in Punch's prescient retirement address—demonstrate a commitment to not only feeding the hungry but to working for food justice and economic equality. Early on, the CFB clearly recognized that this could be achieved only through education and advocacy.

Many other food banks around the country now talk about the need to address the root causes of hunger, using the phrase "shorten the food line" to describe their mission. But from the CFB's earliest days, the ultimate goal was always to *eliminate* the food line and end the need for food banks altogether. Or "put Punch out of business," as he himself often said.

The vision of the Community Food Bank is to eradicate hunger. In light of this vision, our mission is to respond to the food needs of people in southeastern Arizona through education, advocacy and the acquisition, storage, and distribution of food.

—CFB MISSION STATEMENT, 1990

Let's put Punch out of business! Let's not need food banks anymore. Let's put an end to a society where people are hungry, end a need for food boxes, and end a need for food banks to provide those boxes.

—PUNCH WOODS, "PUNCHLINE," MAY/JUNE 1986

Unfortunately, implementing this ambitious goal wasn't easy early on. The daily demand for the CFB's basic services—just feeding the hungry—was all-consuming, and building the means to satisfy that demand as it continued to grow occupied most of the staff's time and energy.

Punch Woods, Former CFB Executive Director

Ending hunger is but one step toward economic justice. It seems obvious to me to say social and economic justice for all is good for everyone. But we tend to consider another's poverty not our problem; another's hunger not our problem; another's sick child not our problem; another's low wages not our problem. Not only is it ethically and morally wrong to dismiss their needs, but it is financially costly to society and to us.

— PUNCH WOODS, FORMER CFB EXECUTIVE DIRECTOR, RETIREMENT ADDRESS, JANUARY 2003

Although we all knew that we needed to do more than provide hunger relief, we didn't have the time and resources to focus on the root causes of the problem. In the early years, we were always underfunded and understaffed. To illustrate, I recall a board president once suggesting to me that I delegate some of what I was doing. I laughed and said, there's no one to give it to!

Looking back, perhaps we could've done more, but what we did do was build a foundation that later would allow the CFB to work toward hunger prevention.

— PUNCH WOODS, FORMER CFB EXECUTIVE DIRECTOR

This, however, began to change shortly after the acquisition of the Punch Woods Multi-Service Center. In 1997, in cooperation with the Community Gardens of Tucson, the CFB broke ground for the Nuestra Tierra Demonstration Garden, which would offer the organization's first major food education program. Located just outside the new headquarters, it was easily accessible to clients picking up their food boxes. Here they could not only see examples of healthy food being grown but, through the classes offered, actually learn how to grow these vegetables in Nuestra Tierra's small garden plots.

This pilot garden project initially had an all-volunteer staff, including individuals who would later become key employees, serving the CFB and its clients for many years.

Nuestra Tierra Demonstration Garden

Varga Garland, Former Director, Community Food Resource Center

I've been a vegetable gardener since I was young. I never ate the first watermelon I grew because I was so proud; I wanted to show it to everyone. Growing food or flowers or homes for insects and birds is a life-expanding experience—gardening expanded my experience of the world.

When I moved to Tucson in the late 1990s, I found the organic gardening community and it led me to the CFB. I worked first as a volunteer, then as a staff person. With the help of an ever-growing and changing force of volunteers, I founded the Community Food Resource Center in the early 2000s.

We began working to make food an issue of justice, not charity. We started with gardening, went on to farmers' markets, farming, and food system education primarily with people with low incomes. Along with Pima Community College Family Literacy, schools, and other community partners, we set out to build a local food system accessible by all incomes and cultures.

—VARGA GARLAND, FORMER DIRECTOR,
COMMUNITY FOOD RESOURCE CENTER

Tuesday Market

A few years later, following up on the success of Nuestra Tierra, the CFB opened an on-site farmers' market, the Tuesday Market. Here, clients and others from the community could purchase fresh, nutritious produce grown by local farmers.

While this was not the first farmers' market in Tucson, and only a limited number of farms initially participated, the concept behind the Tuesday Market would soon bear bountiful fruit. It served as a model for the 2005 establishment of an off-site farmers' market, the Santa Cruz River Farmers' Market in Barrio Hollywood, then as a driving force in the CFB's expansion into agriculture-based education programming, including the installation of home gardens and the development of its own farm, the Marana Heritage Farm, in 2007.

In 2001, with the help of federal and state grants, the Community Food Resource Center (CFRC)—the CFB's most important step in moving beyond hunger relief to food justice—was established. Under the leadership of Varga Garland, Director of the CFRC from 2001 to 2010, the CFRC expanded the CFB's community partnerships and progressive education agenda. At the CFRC, clients learned about growing their own food, eating healthfully, and advocating for themselves. They also received information on how to navigate the often-bewildering system of social services, such as SNAP, available to low-income families.

The CFRC also laid the groundwork for later, more substantial education programming in nutrition, health, and job training, providing clients with not just hope and dignity but the tools needed to improve the overall quality of their lives.

The year 2001 was noteworthy in another respect, one consistent with the goal of making the CFB a family-friendly operation and treating its clients with respect: With help from its volunteers, and funds and materials from KABOOM!, Home Depot, and Tucson Electric Power, a children's playground was built on the grounds of the Multi-Service Center.

Punch Woods retired in 2003, having helped establish a strong foundation for further growth, rooted in the CFB's trademark culture of caring, sharing, and innovating. This foundation was strengthened and diversified in new directions under the leadership of CEO Bill Carnegie (2006–2013).

One bold contribution during Bill Carnegie's tenure was the elimination of all fees on food distributed to the CFB's agency partners. The CFB was one of the first food banks in the country to do this. Another innovative move was the development in 2009 of the Youth Farm Project at the CFB's Marana Heritage Farm. This farm was built from scratch by its director, Varga Garland, and Dana Helfer, the food production manager, and operated with the help of many volunteers.

Playground at Multi-Service Center

Bill Carnegie, Former CFB CEO

I had the pleasure of service as the CFB's CEO from 2006 to 2013. During that time, I was presented with numerous opportunities to build infrastructure, expand services, and move the CFB to the forefront of hunger relief organizations across the country.

I firmly believe the people who work in an organization are its most important asset. Change does not happen because of one person. I was fortunate to work with an incredible staff and board of directors who were dedicated to the mission and vision of the organization.

The CFB has always done a great job of engaging the community and keeping the public aware of what it was doing in the local fight against hunger. People like to give to successful organizations and know that their donations will be invested wisely. The CFB has long been recognized as one of the most progressive food banks in the nation, as it continually raises the bar through innovation, transparency, and compassion.

—BILL CARNEGIE, FORMER CFB CEO

The Youth Farm Project was designed to give teenagers hands-on experience growing their own food. Its success would fuel the later emphasis on education programming for children in several child-nutrition initiatives.

In 2010, the CFB continued its expansion into rural southeastern Arizona by opening new branches in Sahuarita and Nogales. The Nogales branch deserves special mention, as it would later expand greatly and, given its location at the Mexican border, play a pivotal role in helping to bring more fresh produce to those served throughout the region.

At the CFB branch in Nogales, unlike at some pantries, clients select from the food options offered, empowering them to make healthy choices. The CFB is now introducing this model of client choice to other branches, such as Green Valley/Amado.

During Bill Carnegie's tenure, major technical improvements were made at the Multi-Service Center. Warehouse space was increased 300 percent with the installation of push-back racking. Solar power was introduced, and the vehicle fleet expanded to forty-eight, including the use of the first commercial hybrid trucks. A 14,000-gallon rainwater cistern was added, one of the largest in southern Arizona.

Varga Garland (*left*) and Dana Helfer (*right*)
at Marana Heritage Farm

Marana Heritage Farm

Max, Youth Farm Project Participant

I participated in the Youth Farm Project, and it definitely shaped who I've become. It provides an incredible introduction to the world of sustainability and food justice. I think it's really important to Tucson because it creates a space for young people to feel empowered, give back, and learn how to protect the future of their community.

—MAX, PARTICIPANT IN YOUTH
FARM PROJECT

These improvements in capacity and efficiency were all the more noteworthy and essential in that they were made during the Great Recession (2007–2008), when the demand for the CFB's services saw another dramatic spike, and when food insecurity in the United States reached a level not seen since the Great Depression.

During these hard times, there was a commensurate increase in the work force. By 2010, there were about one-hundred staff members, supported by more than 2000 volunteers. Yet increased demand during the Great Recession doesn't fully explain such growth. The fact remains that the CFB also continued to be an extremely well-run, attractive place to work.

It is no wonder, then, that the CFB has remained a model for food banks around the country, and has received numerous awards for its contributions to the community and for the high quality of the organization itself. These awards include the Harry Chapin Self-Reliance Award in 2005 and the Hunger's Hope Award from Feeding America on several occasions.

Client Choice Pantry at CFB's Green Valley Branch

Bill Carnegie with Hybrid Truck at the Multi-Service Center

Push-Back Warehouse Racking at the Multi-Service Center

Rainwater Cistern at the Multi-Service Center

Solar Power Structures at the Multi-Service Center

Beginning in 2008, the CFB has consistently received a 4-Star rating—the highest possible—by Charity Navigator for "sound fiscal management"; for many times in the past several years, it has been voted one of the Best Nonprofits to Work For in America by the *NonProfit Times*. In 2012, Bill Carnegie was named Food Bank Executive Director of the Year by Feeding America.

By the turn of the twenty-first century, the CFB had begun to turn the corner in attacking the fundamental causes of hunger and poverty. The inroads made become more and more evident as the story of the CFB continues to unfold. It's a story not merely of caring and sharing, but of giving the less fortunate the most valuable gift of all: the gift of knowledge. And perhaps it answers a question Punch once asked: "How can we give the greatest gift of all to the poor man, the gift of not needing charity?"

Bill Carnegie, Recipient of Food Bank Executive Director of the Year Award, 2012

PART II

It Takes More Than Food

We change lives in the communities we serve by feeding the hungry and building a healthy, hunger-free tomorrow.

The Challenge:

    (1) Equal Access to Healthy Food

    (2) Serious Diet-Related Diseases

    (3) Social Isolation

    (4) Lack of Economic Opportunity

The Strategy:

To build a healthy, hunger-free environment, we bring together

    (1) Health and Food;

    (2) Education;

    (3) Community Development

-CFB MISSION STATEMENT

CHAPTER 7

THE REVOLUTION AT THE COMMUNITY FOOD BANK OF SOUTHERN ARIZONA

Anticipate charity by preventing poverty.

—MAIMONIDES

IN 2015, UNDER THE LEADERSHIP of its new CEO, Michael McDonald, the CFB embarked on a major restructuring, a process that continues today and undoubtedly will shape the organization's future and that of the larger community it serves. Once again, the CFB is reinventing itself, reexamining its mission and developing new tactics that it hopes will be more effective in attacking the underlying causes of hunger and poverty.

Sadly, the fact remains that, despite sustained efforts, the need today is even greater than when the CFB opened its doors more than forty years ago. In Arizona, about one in five adults and one in four children are food insecure.

As its new mission statement and strategic goals suggest, the emphasis is now on hunger and poverty *prevention*, as well as on the overall well-being of those served. While hunger-relief efforts continue undiminished, education, community development, and advocacy are priorities today. To reinvigorate the CFB's legendary egalitarian spirit and culture of innovation, efforts are being made to develop new programming compatible with these priorities, and to support staff in their role as changemakers in the community.

Michael McDonald, CFB CEO

The CFB began with a desire to change the system. Our co-founders experienced firsthand the indignities of governmental bureaucracy when they needed to use food stamps. Thereafter, they began advocating for a better way to ensure empathy and equity in people's access to a resource that should be a basic human right. People started donating food and funds, and soon we became the region's most respected hunger-relief charity.

But despite decades of feeding hungry people, we haven't fed hunger out of existence. In fact, we've seen the number and percentage of people in need grow from 14 percent of the population in southern Arizona four decades ago to 19 percent of the population today. Thus, the long line of hungry people continues to grow because we haven't adequately attacked the roots of hunger in the structural inequities of poverty.

The recent reorganizing of the CFB has been to return to our origins, re-integrating and strengthening our commitment to both charity and justice. In doing so, we hope to adequately address the persistent lack of access to healthy affordable foods, the often-hidden epidemic of diet-related disease, the individual and societal damage caused by social isolation and the lack of economic mobility and opportunity. We pursue these goals with this in mind: the promise of the American dream exceeds the reach of an increasing majority of hardworking families who are simply trying to make ends meet each and every day.

It's instructive to recall our founder's recitation of the adage that 'what is owed in justice should never be given in charity.'

—MICHAEL MCDONALD, CFB CEO

The Community Food Bank of Southern Arizona is an outstanding organization that is making a big difference in the lives of people facing hunger throughout the region. They are distributing nutritious food—including lots of fresh produce—to struggling communities and supporting people in need to build skills and pursue opportunities that create financial stability and self-sufficiency.

—MATT KNOTT, FORMER PRESIDENT OF FEEDING AMERICA

What is happening before our eyes at the CFB is no mere tweaking of existing operations and programs. In fact, some may say a revolution is in the works. But risk-taking is in the CFB's blood, so perhaps we shouldn't be surprised to see the CFB pursue its new agenda so fearlessly, creatively, and energetically.

There are bound to be challenges when a well-established and otherwise successful organization initiates radical changes—operational disruptions, as well as

Robert Ojeda Accepts Feeding America Member of the Year Award for the CFB, 2018

some resistance from staff, partners, and the greater community. For a new approach to succeed, those in charge of designing and managing it need to communicate its principles clearly and consistently to workers on the ground carrying it out. This is especially difficult to achieve in organizations with a widely dispersed workforce such as the CFB.

The new CFB is not immune to these problems. It is now addressing them, and is doing so in ways consistent with its traditional institutional values and legacy of respect for others and their opinions. As in the early days, debate is encouraged, and feedback from CFB constituents is actively sought by posing the same question the founders always asked: "How can we do it better?"

Today, this evaluation process is far more comprehensive and objective, thanks to the availability of scientific data: namely, the results of CFB-sponsored studies of its staff and operations conducted by University of Arizona anthropologists. These findings help pinpoint where improvements can be made in the CFB's new organizational structure and programming.

Members of the food-banking world are also closely watching the transformation of one of its leaders. Their assessment of progress so far is largely positive. In 2018, for example, Feeding America honored the CFB by naming it Member of the Year. Its president, Matt Knott, applauded the CFB's many contributions to the community over the years and its revolutionary work today.

Hunger is closer than you think.

We assist people across 23,106 square miles of southern Arizona.

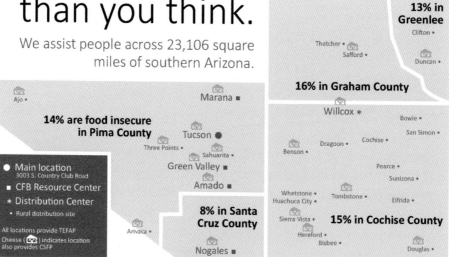

SERVICE AREA MAP

13% in Greenlee

Clifton •

Thatcher •
Safford •
Duncan •

16% in Graham County

Willcox *

14% are food insecure in Pima County

Ajo •

Marana ■

Tucson ●
Three Points •
Sahuarita •

Green Valley ■

Amado ■

Bowie •
San Simon •

Dragoon •
Cochise •

Benson •

Pearce •

Sunizona •

Whetstone •
Huachuca City •
Tombstone •
Elfrida •

Sierra Vista •
15% in Cochise County

Hereford •
Bisbee •
Douglas •

8% in Santa Cruz County

Arivaca •

Nogales ■

● **Main location**
3003 S. Country Club Road

■ **CFB Resource Center**

* **Distribution Center**

• **Rural distribution site**

All locations provide TEFAP
Cheese (🧀) indicates location
also provides CSFP

Map of Community Food Bank service areas
and their at-risk of hunger populations.

Source: Feeding America
*Map the Meal Gap 2018: Overall Food
Insecurity in Arizona by County in 2016*

COMMUNITY FOOD BANK
OF SOUTHERN ARIZONA

MEMBER OF
FEEDING
AMERICA

communityfoodbank.org

CFB Service Area in Southern Arizona

CHAPTER 8

IT TAKES A COMMUNITY

What do we have to live for, if not to make life less difficult for others.
-GEORGE ELIOT

WHO WOULD HAVE IMAGINED THAT a food bank once operating on a shoestring would grow into one with an annual budget now exceeding $125 million? Even more impressive: Of this budget's total, only about three percent goes to administrative and fundraising costs; the rest goes to the CFB's basic operations and its diverse and ever-growing programming. In other words, as little money as food is wasted at this highly efficient organization.

In 2019, the CFB distributed more than 250,000 food boxes to nearly 200,000 families and individuals at its five main locations—Tucson, Green Valley/Amado, Marana, Nogales, and Willcox—and through its 385 agency partners.

When one looks at the amount of *fresh* produce distributed—more than fifty-million pounds or nearly fifty-million servings of vegetables and fruits—it is obvious that the CFB is committed to improving the health of its clients. And it is making inroads at an ever-increasing pace: As the accompanying chart illustrates, the amount of fresh produce distributed in 2018 more than quintupled that distributed in 2015, a testament to the productivity of the CFB's Food Sourcing staff.

Dana Yost, CFB Chief Operations Officer

The primary goal of the CFB's Food Sourcing team is to create a sustainable food supply chain. The key to the tremendous recent growth of our Produce Rescue Program lies in our new approach. Since I came aboard in 2016, we've moved from a model emphasizing charity to a pure business model, where the salvaging of food is presented to suppliers as being in their best economic interest. We make it logistically practical and financially prudent for growers and distributors not to dump their produce. By working with us to save it, they save money.

—DANA YOST, CFB CHIEF OPERATIONS OFFICER

Client Mix, 2019

Growth in the Amount of Fresh Produce Distributed

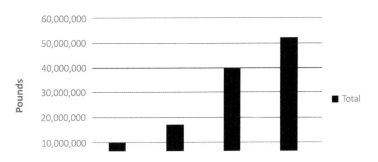

Growth in the Amount of Fresh Produce Distributed, 2015–2019

Kara Jones, CFB Director of
Partnerships and Community
Impact

*I lead the team that builds and maintains nearly 400
food distribution partnerships with nonprofit, public, and
faith-based organizations that distribute food to people in
need. The CFB is well positioned to obtain high volumes of
commodity foods, donated food, and produce, but we rely on
partner organizations to distribute about half of that food—
and these organizations, rooted in various communities, are
better suited at getting this emergency food to people in their
areas, and often offering additional support services as well.*

*In the coming years, we'd like to play a larger role
in strengthening the connections between these partner
organizations. Further developing our network of organizations that support families in multiple
ways opens up opportunities for coordinated services and even collective impact.*

*I do this work because I truly believe that community groups and anchor institutions can
change the systems that create injustices—that collectively we can imagine a different future and
act together to make it a reality.*

—KARA JONES, CFB DIRECTOR OF PARTNERSHIPS
AND COMMUNITY IMPACT

Meal at Cross Streets Community

The CFB today continues to rely heavily on its partner organizations to meet the needs of the hungry. The number of such agencies also continues to grow in step with the ever-increasing demand. The work entailed in organizing this large, highly diverse distribution network presents challenges that the founders never faced. Getting food to 200,000 people is no simple task. Yet the CFB has responded, as usual, with creative solutions.

While the CFB's strategies have changed, its client base today differs little from that of the early days: The majority are still the working poor, children, and seniors.

This isn't to say the homeless have been forgotten. To illustrate the continuing commitment to their welfare, consider the CFB's contribution to the members of the Cross Streets Community: A Ministry of Southside Presbyterian Church, a longtime leader in the social justice and sanctuary movements.

For many years, the ministry's dedicated volunteers, such as Doug Larson, have been providing food, clothing, and other services to this homeless community. Cross Streets today serves 30,000 meals a year, and this food supplied by the CFB is now more varied and much more healthful than ever before.

The problems encountered by immigrants crossing our southern border are well known today. Many end up in Tucson and neighboring towns. Helping them is one of the main priorities of Casa San Juan, another faith-based agency served by the CFB. Each month at Casa San Juan, hundreds of families receive medical assistance, emergency food, and help with shelter and clothing.

The creation of the Cross Streets Community began twenty years ago. It has grown immensely to serve our neighbors in need in the Barrio of West Ochoa.

We have no paid staff. Yet, thanks to over 30,000 cumulative volunteer hours of work, we served 30,000 meals last year, distributed 10,000 pieces of clothing, provided 3,000 hot showers and 700 haircuts, and spent numerous hours with visitations at jails and hospitals. Through the CFB we picked up ten tons of food from Trader Joe's alone, over 2,200 pounds of pastries from Starbucks, 1,800 pounds of pizza from Pizza Hut, and 230 pounds of prepared meats from Chipotle. In addition, the CFB delivers one to two pallets of fresh produce every other week to the church's door.

None of this could happen without the unwavering support of the CFB. It provides not only the food but also the guidance in food safety, training, and conferences, and the ability to collaborate with other organizations in our barrio and region that have similar purposes. Food is necessary, but we believe that even more so it is the catalyst that brings people from all walks of life together for one purpose—to learn from each other and demonstrate true compassionate love.

—DR. DOUGLAS LARSON, PROGRAM DIRECTOR, CROSS STREETS COMMUNITY

Casa San Juan

Many of the people we serve are migrants. Without the food we supply, they would starve for who knows how long. One woman came in with her four children. They were about to be evicted. They hadn't eaten, and when we gave them food, she started crying.

I have nothing but appreciation for the food bank. Without them, Casa San Juan might not exist.

—PATRICIA ARTEGA, DIRECTOR OF CASA SAN JUAN

National Distribution of Fresh Produce in Feeding America Network

The geographical reach of the CFB today is extremely impressive. Its service network now covers 23,000 square miles in five counties of southern Arizona: Pima, Santa Cruz, Graham, Greenlee, and Cochise. And the distribution network is much larger, extending far beyond southern Arizona. Through the CFB's Produce Rescue Program, about 500,000 tons of fresh produce are rescued annually and distributed to twenty-six states in the Feeding America food bank system.

About a third of all produce in America is grown in or travels through Arizona. Working with about 230 produce brokers and wholesalers at the Nogales entry port, as well as with growers in Mexico, the CFB's Food Sourcing team helps coordinate this nationwide distribution. The success of this effort would not be possible without the work of the Nogales Resource Center, which provides essential logistical assistance. Nor would it be possible without the cooperation of such Food Rescue Program partners as the Mexican grower and shipper Wilson Produce, a recipient of the Hunger Hero award.

Our location near the Mexican border and the rich agricultural resources to the south give the CFB an opportunity that few food banks have. We have taken full advantage of it in developing our Food Rescue Program. Our far-reaching salvaged food distribution network also helps spread the word about what else we're achieving today as a changemaker. This attention, in turn, makes it easier for us to advance our new agenda, particularly our complementary fresh, healthy food initiative.

— DANA YOST, CFB CHIEF OPERATIONS OFFICER

Willcox Distribution Center, 2019 (Russell Varineau)

Drive-Through Pantry at Willcox Distribution Center, 2019 (Russell Varineau)

Another key to the success of the CFB's geographic expansion was the establishment in 2015 of the Willcox Distribution Center, initially under the management of Joy Tucker. Developed with a $1.2-million grant from the Howard G. Buffett Foundation and designed as the distribution hub for rural southeastern Arizona, this 8,000-square-foot facility serves clients at brick-and-mortar and mobile pantries in twenty-seven communities in Graham, Greenlee, and Cochise counties, such as the towns of Benson, Bisbee, and Douglas.

Located in the heart of southeastern Arizona's richest agricultural area, the Willcox Distribution Center has a staff of five, aided by many volunteers. Here you'll find state-of-the-art climate control and food-safety systems for the most efficient storage and distribution of food. Staff and volunteers also distribute food boxes and fresh produce to local residents on a monthly basis, and in a distinctive way: Clients pick up food in their own vehicles, creating what could be called a drive-through pantry.

I've worked at the Willcox Distribution Center since it opened and it's a real busy place. During growing season, we process about five-million pounds of produce from both local farms and the Nogales entry port.

I like the work because it's not only challenging but more rewarding than any other I've done in warehousing and transportation. There's nothing better than helping others and seeing how much families appreciate what we give them.

One of my favorite parts of the job is mixing different sorts of food in the boxes to give clients greater variety. It's much easier to do now that we have so many more types of fresh vegetables and fruits to distribute.

—HOMERO GOMEZ, FORMER MANAGER, WILLCOX DISTRIBUTION CENTER

Homero Gomez at Willcox Distribution Center, 2019 (Russell Varineau)

Ben Johnson at Tombstone Pantry, 2019 (Russell Varineau)

I'd been to Tombstone a few times on vacation and liked it: the climate, interesting history and friendly people. So when I retired from my job as an air-conditioning contractor, I decided to live here. A friend told me about the food bank and a few years ago, wanting to do something useful, I began volunteering. At that time, I could see that it wasn't being run as well as it could and that many visitors weren't happy with the service and the atmosphere.

Most of our clients live on a small fixed income, often not enough to make ends meet. I've tried to help them by making our pantry operate better and be a friendlier place to visit. We're now putting in a covered patio where clients can sit and talk with each other. Our food bank has become a sort of senior center. It makes me feel good that I can help those not as lucky as me.

— BEN JOHNSON, VOLUNTEER DIRECTOR, TOMBSTONE FOOD BANK

In many ways, the Tombstone Food Bank is typical of those in Cochise County supplied by the Willcox Distribution Center. It, too, serves a largely rural small population. Yet the "Town Too Tough to Die" has its own unique character, and not just because it's a famous Old West tourist destination. What tourists don't see when watching a reenactment of the O.K. Corral gunfight or visiting Boothill Graveyard is this community's poverty: About half of its 2,600 permanent residents now receive food boxes, and these people are typically seniors.

Led by its volunteer director, Ben Johnson, the Tombstone Food Bank has recently amped up its services to help these seniors and other food-insecure residents. Its hours of operation have expanded, and food boxes designed specifically for seniors have recently been introduced.

With the aid of twenty-five part-time volunteers, Ben has not only improved this pantry's effectiveness, but made it a more inviting place to visit. In fact, it has become a popular place for often-lonely seniors to socialize with their neighbors. In helping to reduce social isolation, the Tombstone Food Bank fills another important need, one frequently overlooked in the fight against hunger and poverty.

The CFB's older branches are also experiencing growth and implementing change as they, too, develop hunger- and poverty-prevention programs. Located just a few miles northwest of Tucson, the food bank that has for many years served the Town of Marana and the nearby communities of Avra Valley, Oro Valley, Picture Rocks, Rillito, and Cortaro is a good model for the type of progress achievable today at all the CFB's branches.

Its staff of five, assisted by about one-hundred volunteers, serve 2,100 clients monthly, providing them with 1.2-million pounds of food annually. But their clients now receive much more than food. While Marana's population has grown dramatically in recent years—25 percent in the past five—and new suburban housing developments and shopping centers abound, the surrounding area still retains its agricultural economic base and rural flavor. Ironically, high-quality fresh food isn't readily available to Marana's low-income residents. They, like the poor in other areas of rural southeastern Arizona, suffer from food insecurity, chronic health problems, social isolation, and a lack of economic opportunity.

Toward rectifying these problems and transforming itself as an agent of change, Marana's food bank expanded substantially in 2017. With $80,000 from a Pima County Community Development Block Grant and $100,000 from private donations, a 3,000-square-foot facility

Expanded Marana Resource Center, 2018

was added to the existing building. In this much larger space, now shared with such compatible social service organizations as Interfaith Community Services and MHC Healthcare, clients can take advantage of a new job resource center with a computer lab. Here, they are also given help with medical supplies and with applications for food assistance through the Arizona Department of Economic Security and the federal SNAP program. Classes are also offered in cooking, nutrition, General Education Development (GED), and English as a Second Language (ESL).

Is it any wonder, then, that Marana's food bank is now called a *resource* center (the Marana Resource Center), as are all the CFB's branches today?

Linda Hampton, Executive Director,
Marana Resource Center

The story of Betty illustrates how the Marana Resource Center's expanded facilities have improved the lives of those we serve. Betty told me that she did not normally need our help, but now did, having to take care of her grandchildren who'd be spending summer days with her because of the astronomical cost of childcare.

Summer in southern Arizona brings unique problems to families. Utility bills skyrocket. People with service jobs often experience a decrease in hours as winter visitors leave. Difficult choices about paying bills or buying food must sometimes be made.

As I chatted with Betty, I learned that she would benefit from services available through other agencies. Fortunately, these agencies are now located within the Marana Resource Center. Our partnerships have made critical care available to the surrounding community. In most cases, these services did not previously exist here and traveling to Tucson to get help was not an option for some of our rural families.

Our mission statement begins with 'We change lives.' In Marana, we don't take that as a suggestion; to us it is a mandate. It is wonderful to see Betty now and know that she is receiving emergency food and has solutions to other problems as well.

—LINDA HAMPTON, EXECUTIVE DIRECTOR, MARANA RESOURCE CENTER

📍 Ocotillo Early Learning Center
📍 Drexel Elementary School
📍 Elvira Elementary School
📍 Santa Clara Elementary School
📍 Summit View Elementary School

📍 Los Amigos Technology Academy
📍 Apollo Middle School
📍 Challenger Middle School
📍 Desert View High School
📍 Sunnyside High School

Local Schools in Farm to School Program

CHAPTER 9

IT TAKES EDUCATION

Education is the most powerful weapon which you can use to change the world.
–NELSON MANDELA

IT SHOULD BE CLEAR THAT many resources are needed in the fight against hunger and poverty in our communities. Perhaps the single most effective resource is education. Sadly, despite what we hear routinely from our government leaders, not enough is being done to make education a high priority, particularly in a state like Arizona where the need is great.

At the CFB, however, providing clients with education/advocacy services *is* now a major priority. In 2017, nearly 20,000 community members, including 7,500 children, benefited from the CFB's education outreach programs in gardening, cooking, and nutrition. Through the years, more than fifty local schools have partnered with the CFB in its Farm to Child Program to support healthy eating.

This emphasis on empowering children is especially important in light of the actual need: One-in-four kids in Arizona are at risk of hunger, and about a third of the CFB's emergency food recipients are children. The aim of the Farm to Child Program is to give these children from low-income families not just healthier food, but the hands-on gardening experience and nutrition knowledge children need to be able to advocate for themselves, and thus cultivate the right habits to ensure good health later in life. At elementary schools in Tucson, such as Borton and Manzo, the CFB has helped the teachers and their students establish vegetable gardens and install irrigation, aquaponic, and composting systems.

Molly Courtney, Teacher, in Garden at Borton Elementary School

The garden is a way to show kids that what you're learning in the classroom connects with everything outside. It's a way to help them become involved in the community. None of it would be here if we didn't have support from our families, our school community, volunteers, and the CFB's Farm to School Program.

— MOLLY COURTNEY, TEACHER AT BORTON ELEMENTARY SCHOOL

Robert Ojeda, CFB Chief Program Officer

Prevention is the best recipe for eliminating diet-related diseases in the communities we serve. By reinforcing nutrition education principles during their vital formative years, children have the potential to develop healthy habits for life. By providing nutrition education to children, we are creating opportunities for them to live healthy and productive lives. These children, in turn, will drive broader and lasting change.

—ROBERT OJEDA, CFB CHIEF PROGRAM OFFICER

Educating children in this respect is perhaps the most vital contribution the CFB can make as an agent of meaningful, enduring change in the community. With this in mind, the CFB strives to improve its existing education programs, such as the child-nutrition initiative, and to develop related ones.

Manzo Elementary School Children Harvesting Chard

The larger goal of community education—improving diet and health while reducing poverty—underlies the development of the Farm to Child Program. This program expands on the educational concept behind the pioneering Kids Cafe Program—now called After School Meals & Snacks.

The CFB today supports twenty-two After School Meals & Snacks sites, and is currently working with ten schools with the goal of serving produce grown in their own gardens. The continued dramatic growth of the Farm to Child Program—one that holds great promise in offering children a brighter, healthier future—seems likely.

Putting the Farm to Child Program into operation wasn't quick and easy; the CFB had to overcome numerous bureaucratic obstacles. That it persevered and succeeded testifies to the CFB's commitment as an advocate for the needy in the public policy arena.

Equally challenging were the CFB's more recent efforts to obtain match funding for SNAP at the state government level. Working with legislators for more than a year, and in partnership with the nonprofit Pinnacle Prevention, CFB staff finally succeeded in 2018 in getting SB 1245—the SNAP Fresh Fruit and Vegetable Incentive—passed.

Marco Liu, Former CFB Director of
Family Advocacy and Outreach

My first encounter with the CFB was back in 1981 as an Arizona Department of Economic Security caseworker, picking up food boxes for food stamp applicants whose eligibility determination would take one to three weeks or longer, but who needed food that day. It was then that I learned how the CFB was a critical part of a larger hunger-relief system. This was a seminal experience for me and led to a career in hunger relief and prevention that has spanned thirty-eight years. With the restructuring of the CFB, my primary focus shifted to advocacy and public policy.

My work with the CFB has been rewarding, as it has closely aligned with the agency mission, which has inspired me. Equally meaningful has been the privilege of working with colleagues who have both supported me and challenged me in ways that have given me a great deal of personal fulfillment.

—MARCO LIU, FORMER CFB DIRECTOR OF FAMILY ADVOCACY
AND OUTREACH

The direct relationship between income, diet, and health is now well established; we know that the incidence of chronic diseases like diabetes, obesity, and high blood pressure is higher among the poor. The CFB's Food Safari Nutrition Education Program addresses these health risks head on. Nutrition science undergraduates from the University of Arizona teach the Food Safari curriculum to children at the CFB's After School Meals & Snacks sites. About 2,000 children participate today in this rapidly growing education program.

Food Safari Class, 2018

Their faces light up with excitement when they see us preparing for the Food Safari lesson. It's an amazing feeling to know that I'm having a positive impact on children in our community.

—GABRIEL CASTILLO, FORMER FOOD SAFARI GUIDE

Family Volunteer Day

Gardening Workshop at Nuestra Tierra
Learning Garden, 2013

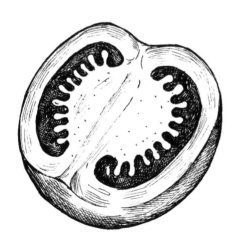

With much the same long-term goal in mind, the CFB introduced an educational initiative called the School Pantry Program, which relies on the participation of parents. In a related program, Cooking Matters at the Store—part of the federal SNAP-Ed curriculum—clients are taken to nearby grocery stores where, under the guidance of a trained facilitator, they learn how to identify healthy foods, read labels, compare unit prices, and shop for affordable produce.

Family Volunteer Day perhaps best captures the essence of the CFB's commitment to education and the role of sharing in creating a healthy community. In 2017, more than 400 children, families, and school groups attended the event and learned about hunger and nutrition while working with their neighbors in the warehouse and the garden.

Not surprisingly in light of the CFB's current priorities, the Garden Workshops have also expanded greatly in recent years, both at the original Nuestra Tierra Demonstration Garden site on the grounds of the Multi-Service Center— now called Nuestra Tierra Learning Garden— and at Las Milpitas Community Farm.

Nuestra Tierra Learning Garden no longer provides gardening plots to clients and nearby residents. This community service is offered instead by the CFB's Las Milpitas Community Farm. As its new name suggests, Nuestra Tierra *Learning* Garden today focuses primarily on teaching people about desert food production, rainwater harvesting, container gardening, composting, and using organic fertilizers such as worm casings. In 2017, 3,283 people attended 166 CFB-sponsored workshops on backyard gardening and healthy eating.

Developed in 2011 to replace the Marana Heritage Farm, Las Milpitas is a six-acre community farm operated by the CFB for the benefit of low-income residents of the nearby Santa Cruz neighborhood, as well as qualifying individuals living elsewhere. Located within the city of Tucson along the Santa Cruz River, it offers, at no cost, family garden plots, supplies, and educational workshops.

In 2018, Las Milpitas members grew 4, 352 pounds of produce in sixty-eight garden plots. The farm hosted students from ten local schools, provided eighteen free gardening workshops, held a weeklong camp for local children, and introduced a just-for-kids interactive space called the Learning Garden. Las Milpitas also supplies fresh produce and eggs to the CFB's farmers' markets and its Caridad Community Kitchen.

As is the case with the CFB's other community development programs, Las Milpitas' operations are carried out largely by its volunteers—120 in 2018—under the supervision of a small paid staff. The goal, apart from providing healthy food to those in need, is to help community members help themselves by creating a sustainable neighborhood food system.

Las Milpitas Community Farm

Melissa Mundt, Former CFB Farm and
Garden Manager

On an early spring day, I was rinsing just-harvested collard greens from Nuestra Tierra Learning Garden. A woman who had just come through the food box line came to the garden. She was visibly frazzled, and I welcomed her to explore the garden. She said she had just moved from Louisiana, that things had been really stressful, but that she would love to get a garden going at her new place.

I let her know about the free classes and supplies we could provide. Then she noticed what I was doing, and her face lit up as she told me about her family's collard green recipe and how much she missed those flavors. I handed her a bunch to take and she burst into happy tears.

The food she received in her food box was essential for her, but I think her time in the garden and getting those greens was nourishing for her heart.

— MELISSA MUNDT, FORMER CFB
FARM AND GARDEN MANAGER

Community gardens like Las Milpitas are especially important to Tucson's many renters, particularly those living in apartment complexes without access to suitable gardening plots. Monica Velasco lives in one, but that hasn't stopped her.

Originally from Oaxaca, Mexico, Monica has been a garden member at Las Milpitas for the past three years. Her garden plot, and the workshops she has taken in healthy eating, irrigation, and composting have made a big difference in the quality of her life and that of her three children. Las Milpitas has also given her a community of like-minded individuals and families she otherwise lacks.

The CFB is widely recognized among the nation's food banks as a pioneer and major innovator in the areas of urban gardening and nutrition education.

After Nuestra Tierra was established, I happened to look out my office window and saw a mother and two boys enjoying the garden. Mom was leaning on the fence, looking at the vegetables. She was pointing at different ones, showing and telling her boys what was what.

Wonderful, passive learning— exactly what was designed to happen!

— PUNCH WOODS, FORMER CFB
EXECUTIVE DIRECTOR

Elena Ortiz, Former Las Milpitas Farm
Community Engagement and Advocacy
Coordinator

At Las Milpitas, we teach community members how to grow food organically in the desert and how to engage with others on matters related to community health. I see my role as being a facilitator, trainer, and convener. I facilitate farm work days with fellow Milpitas staff to give community gardeners and outside volunteers hands-on experience with an approach to gardening that cares for people and the earth. I train interns and Garden Leaders on basic desert gardening and also leadership skills, such as facilitating meetings and communicating about our program to the Greater Tucson community.

As a native Tucsonan, I'm committed to working with the community for a healthier and more equitable Tucson. I didn't grow up gardening or having a close relationship with food. It was my desire to live a more sustainable lifestyle that taught me about the waste and destruction caused by parts of our food system. In an effort to make a difference, I started learning how to grow my own food and started supporting local farmers. Through this experience, I've seen how unequal access to healthy food is in our community, a reality that makes me angry and fuels my work. Through our work at the CFB, however, I'm finding that food can indeed heal people and bring us together to build community.

—ELENA ORTIZ, FORMER LAS MILPITAS FARM COMMUNITY
ENGAGEMENT AND ADVOCACY COORDINATOR

I first heard of Las Milpitas while involved with the group Paisanos Unidos, which had a garden plot there. I grew up in the city in Oaxaca and had little gardening experience. At Las Milpitas, I've learned how to grow all kinds of organic vegetables, but I love chiles and tomatoes the most. Growing and eating healthy food is very important to me because my family suffers from diabetes. I've also made many new friends there who I not only work with but socialize with now. Las Milpitas has changed my life!

—MONICA VELASCO, LAS MILPITAS GARDEN MEMBER

School Group Visits Las Milpitas Community Farm

Encouraging leadership in community development, such as at Las Milpitas, is another emphasis of the CFB today. Toward this end, the Garden Leaders program was introduced recently. Garden Leaders work toward completion of a Sustainable Desert Gardening Certification, which gives them advanced skills in, for example, the areas of seed saving, integrated pest management and water conservation. Their knowledge is then shared with members of the local community and applied in the construction of community gardens.

In 2016, the CFB helped install fourteen gardens in public spaces. When neighbors come together to work in these gardens, they grow not only vegetables, but also community pride. They share a sense of achievement, while making both themselves and their communities healthier and more productive.

Isabel Ortiz-Montelong Goodson, a volunteer with the CFB since 2016, is a Garden Leader. One of her most interesting and productive projects was working with residents of the Nottinghill Apartments in Tucson to restore their community garden. She took the lead in organizing several work days and facilitating workshops on irrigation and the use of compost.

My most memorable experience as a volunteer Garden Leader was working alongside refugees, veterans, and low-income families to revitalize the abandoned Nottinghill Garden. We turned it into a green, bountiful organic garden for the whole community. Children and the elderly joined together to learn about sustainable and healthy practices when growing their own food. Participating in this project was especially meaningful to me, as I plan to return to college and hope to make this my life's work.

—ISABEL ORTIZ-MONTELONG GOODSON, CFB GARDEN LEADER

The related volunteer Ambassador Program, introduced in 2016, takes leadership in community development a step further by advocating for social justice and economic change. Volunteers are given in-depth training in the CFB's mission and approaches to issues of health and diet, and the continuing problems of hunger and poverty. They then go out into the community to spread the word of what the CFB is doing to improve the lives of those it serves.

In 2016, seventeen Ambassadors, participating in fifty community events, were able to reach thousands of people in southern Arizona who might have been familiar with these problems of hunger and poverty, but were perhaps unaware of their true extent or the CFB's renewed and expanded efforts to rectify them.

Elaine Lim, CFB Ambassador

My first exposure to the concept of a food bank came during high school when Punch Woods came to speak to my social studies class. The idea that there were so many out there living in need was eye-opening. Since then, social issues have been in the forefront of my consciousness. After college I joined the Peace Corps.

Through the years, the CFB became an important part of my life—first as a volunteer, helping with special events, working in the pantry and making sack lunches at the Caridad Community Kitchen—and more recently as an Ambassador. The Ambassador Program has provided me with a greater insight and understanding of the work of the CFB and the people it serves.

As an Ambassador, I have been proud to represent the CFB at tabling events throughout the community, talking to people and letting them know the many facets of this amazing organization. People tend to think that the CFB is just the food box, but it is so much more!

—ELAINE LIM, CFB AMBASSADOR

Early Community Garden at Quincie Douglas Center

The Ambassador Program is designed to give individuals already volunteering the opportunity for deeper engagement in CFB programmatic and administrative functions and activities. For example, we have had Ambassadors support our development department, monitor agency partners for compliance, and engage in voter registration, community organizing, and advocacy work.

—MARCO LIU, FORMER CFB DIRECTOR OF FAMILY ADVOCACY AND OUTREACH

The CFB charted the way for many food banks, not only in Arizona but across the nation, by venturing into urban gardening and seeing ways to improve nutrition and the availability of the best food for hungry people of all ages, in all types of communities. I am grateful to have been a part of their amazing and successful work to move southern Arizona closer to being hunger-free.

—GINNY HILDEBRAND, FORMER DIRECTOR OF
THE ASSOCIATION OF ARIZONA FOOD BANKS

The Farm to Institution Program is another essential element of the CFB's expanded community development agenda. It provides support to small local farms, which increases their economic security and the region's healthy food supply, thereby keeping resources within the community. In 2016, the CFB helped eighteen local farms sell more than 12,500 pounds to institutions such as Tucson Unified School District and Tucson Medical Center.

John Rueb, Owner, Forever Yong Farms

The CFB's mission isn't that different from ours—we want to get healthy, local food to everyone, regardless of economic class. It's a natural partnership. We're providing good, local food to large markets, and we're able to support our farm.

—JOHN RUEB, OWNER, FOREVER YONG FARMS

The CFB encourages other local nonprofits to participate in this community-building effort by providing them with grants to develop education programs compatible with its own. In 2016, five such nonprofits were awarded a total of $19,000 from the Punch Woods Endowment Grant program.

One recipient, Desert Harvesters, is developing a cookbook and resource guide to educate the public on how to make better use of arid-land foods. Iskashitaa Refugee Network, another recipient of this grant, helps United Nations refugees integrate into the community, offering them, for example, the opportunity to learn English and meet people while harvesting fruit.

We have United Nations refugees who have only been in the country for a few days volunteering to harvest fruit. They're learning English, meeting people, sharing cultural knowledge, going home with food to feed their families—and donating a lot of that food back to local food banks.

I got that call from the CFB, and I called up one of our interns and offered him a job on the spot! It has totally changed how we've been able to serve our community.

— BARBARA EISWERTH, CEO, ISKASHITAA REFUGEE NETWORK

Members of Desert Harvesters at Work

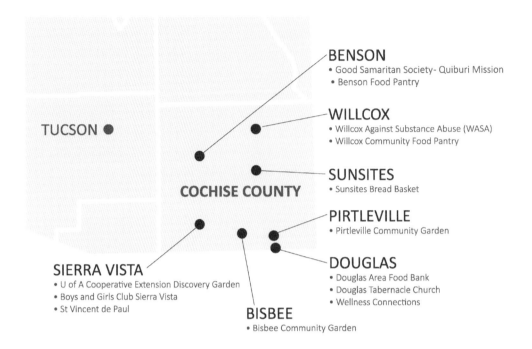

Cochise County Capacity-Building Grantees

In partnership with the Legacy Foundation of Southeast Arizona, which provided a $500,000 three-year grant, the CFB in 2016 awarded a total of $103,000 to twelve nonprofits in Cochise County to increase access to healthy food and improve overall health for low-income residents in seven rural communities.

Diet-related disease is common in Cochise County, where more than three-quarters of client households live below the Federal Poverty Level. In 2017, an additional ten nonprofits in Cochise County received capacity-building grants totaling more than $200,000. This grant money is being used for such community development projects as constructing greenhouses, running cooking and nutrition classes, and providing diabetic food boxes and hot meals for the homeless.

The CFB's increased emphasis on providing healthy food to its clients, as well as the increased efficiency of its various food salvage programs, can be readily seen when one visits the Multi-Service Center and the pantries of the organization's agency partners and satellite branches. At these sites, we see an abundance of fresh vegetables and fruits distributed regularly to supplement the emergency food boxes and Food Plus packages. The food boxes, too, are now being redesigned with chronic disease prevention in mind.

The expansion of the CFB's farmers' markets illustrates this welcome development even more dramatically. Many more local farms now participate, offering a much greater quantity and variety of their seasonal produce at the two CFB markets: the Multi-Service Center's Tuesday Market and the Santa Cruz River Farmers' Market at Mercado San Agustin. Up until 2017, the Kids Farmers' Market also operated in Nogales.

Anyone who regularly visits the Santa Cruz River Farmers' Market will know the stand operated by Alan Robbs—especially if they love pistachios. Alan owns Robbs Family Farm near Willcox. His dad was one of the first to grow pistachios commercially in Arizona. Their forty-acre grove now produces some of the finest nuts in the state.

Volunteer Loads Food Cart with Watermelon

Regular visitors will also be familiar with the many beautiful organic vegetables featured at the stands operated by the CFB at their farmers' markets. This fresh produce comes from local backyard gardeners. The CFB has represented about 150 of them.

Tucson Village Farm Stand at Santa Cruz River Farmers' Market (Kathleen Dreier Photography)

CFB's Tuesday Market Stand

Robbs Family Farm Stand at Santa Cruz River Farmers' Market, 2019
(Russell Varineau)

The Santa Cruz River Farmers' Market gained national recognition when it was named in the *Farmer's Almanac* as one of 10 Farmers' Markets You Need to Visit in 2020.

The larger community benefits in many ways from the growth of the CFB's farmers' markets. First, and perhaps most importantly, the markets are strategically located in neighborhoods that are "food deserts"—areas where low-income residents traditionally have limited access to high-quality fresh foods—thus making it convenient for locals to improve their diets.

The CFB goes a step further in encouraging the purchase of healthy food by offering the Double-Up SNAP incentive at its markets: Buyers using SNAP benefits get up to $20 in a free match when they purchase locally-grown produce. A recent evaluation by University of Arizona researchers of clients using the Double-Up SNAP incentive suggests it increases their awareness of farmers' markets and their consumption of fresh produce.

Providing greater access to nutritious food, while essential, is only part of the CFB's response to the challenges of building a healthy community. Clients have other equally important needs that, for a variety of reasons, often are not satisfied by existing social service and behavioral health agencies. Filling these gaps, either with its own resources or through community partnerships, is another priority of today's CFB.

Building on its Community Food Resource Center's pioneering efforts to provide clients with such help, the CFB in 2012 established the Gabrielle Giffords Family Assistance Center; it was later renamed the Gabrielle Giffords Resource Center. It was made possible with $216,000 donated from forty-eight states and several countries to the Gabrielle Giffords Hunger Action Fund, following the tragic shooting of Arizona Congresswoman Giffords.

Abigail Plano, CFB's Farmers Market Coordinator

My position as the Farmers' Market Coordinator really unites my professional background in social work and one of my personal passions of eating healthy, while supporting our local food system. I love supporting community members, discovering new fruits and vegetables, and getting to know the communities that we serve through sharing recipes and food traditions. I feel lucky to engage with farmers every week!

— ABIGAIL PLANO, CFB
FARMERS' MARKET
COORDINATOR

Conveniently located on the grounds of the Multi-Service Center, adjacent to the food distribution area, the Gabrielle Giffords Resource Center offers clients one-on-one bilingual help in obtaining SNAP benefits and cash and medical assistance from the Department of Economic Security, as well as rent, utility, and prescription drug relief. As part of the CFB's restructuring, plans are now in the works to the make the Gabrielle Giffords Resource Center even more visitor-friendly and responsive to the social service needs of its clients.

Client Talks with Caseworker at Gabrielle Giffords Resource Center

Gabrielle Giffords Resource Center, 2012

In Tucson and southern Arizona, where Spanish is the native language of many residents, access to these federal welfare programs—and, more generally, economic opportunity—is often hindered by a lack of proficiency in speaking and writing English. In recognition of this problem, the CFB, in partnership with the Tucson nonprofit Literacy Connects, is now offering English as a Second Language (ESL) classes at the Multi-Service Center.

Substance abuse has reached epidemic proportions in the United States, and southern Arizona is no exception. The CFB has recently begun to participate in efforts to combat this insidious health problem in local communities. In 2015, at the Douglas Area Food Bank—a partner agency—the CFB worked with Wellness Connections, an organization that offers substance abuse–recovery programs and mental-health services. Wellness Connections was one of the first recipients of the CFB's capacity-building grants in Cochise County.

Chris Mazzarella, Manager, Gabrielle
Giffords Resource Center

I began volunteering at the CFB in January of 2008 and was hired about eighteen months later. I now manage the Gabrielle Giffords Resource Center, where we're working to serve our community in deep, impactful ways that are meaningful and long-lasting.

My time at the CFB has been transformative for me and the communities I've worked with. I've seen eyes light up with new knowledge and understanding; I've seen communities stand taller and advocate for what they need; I've seen people change from one moment to the next as they get the assistance they need. For me, trying to change the world isn't done by bandaging problems. It's done through relationships, education, and justice, and I get to help change the world, one day at a time, using all those tools and more. To me, my work means hope.

—CHRIS MAZZARELLA, MANAGER, GABRIELLE GIFFORDS
RESOURCE CENTER

Wellness Connections at Douglas Food Bank

I believe the food bank and Wellness Connections are all about sharing. Sharing food or information, what we know, what we can do. If we share whatever we have, we can achieve a lot of things.

—MARCIELA, WELLNESS CONNECTIONS

All these programs go a long way toward improving the overall health and well-being of the less fortunate among us. Yet are they enough to make the fundamental changes needed to break the cycle of poverty in our communities?

CHAPTER 10

IT TAKES JOBS

Lack of education, old age, bad health or discrimination—these are the causes of poverty, and the way to attack it is to go to the root.

–ROBERT KENNEDY

PROVIDING GREATER ECONOMIC OPPORTUNITY FOR its clients is one of the CFB's most important contributions as a changemaker. Yet achieving such opportunity is perhaps the most complex challenge faced today, requiring sustained participation by many segments of the community.

The role of the CFB's farmers' markets in economic development illustrates how such progress can be made at the community level. These markets now provide a substantial and diverse supply of fresh fruits and vegetables. Local growers and consumers, including the CFB's clients, obviously benefit from the growth of these markets.

The challenge backyard gardeners and small-scale farmers face is pricing their high-quality produce competitively. The CFB created the Abundant Harvest Cooperative (AHC) to even the playing field and help small producers sell their fresh, chemical-free produce at an affordable price, one within reach of everyone, especially clients. And it's working: In 2017, about 25,000 people purchased food at the CFB's farmers' markets, which benefited 175 local producers.

Lasting solutions to the problems of hunger and poverty depend on the opportunities people have to improve their lives. Workforce development and job training allow folks to build the intellectual, social, and financial capital necessary to be successful.

—ROBERT OJEDA, CFB
CHIEF PROGRAM OFFICER

The Abundant Harvest Cooperative (AHC) is a network of backyard gardeners and small farmers who sell produce through a shared table at weekly farmers' markets run by the CFB. AHC uses an innovative model to provide low-risk economic opportunities for small-scale food producers, while simultaneously making fresh, local produce accessible to low-income customers. In addition to facilitating the sale of locally produced food, AHC also creates spaces for its members to come together to share knowledge and resources, and to build community.

—AUDRA CHRISTOPHEL, CFB LOCAL
FOOD PATHWAYS MANAGER

Abundant Harvest Cooperative Food Stand at Santa Cruz River Farmers' Market

Val Steinbronn, Owner, Vallee Girl Farms

I began growing vegetables with my grandmother when I was growing up in Tucson. As I got older, I continued to always have a garden to grow some of my own food. After I graduated from college, I decided to expand my small garden. Soon I sometimes had too many vegetables to eat! So, in 2011, I began participating in the CFB's consignment program at their Marana Heritage Farm site.

My participation, like the size of my garden, gradually increased, and I started Vallee Girl Farms. I found it rewarding that I could sell my vegetables to locals who shopped at the CFB's farmers markets. French breakfast radishes and brassica salad greens are my favorite vegetables to grow. As the consignment program developed into the Abundant Harvest Cooperative (AHC), I began to participate as a lead grower to help build the foundation of the AHC and create a community of backyard gardeners and farmers.

I have enjoyed learning from other growers, sharing my knowledge, and forming lasting relationships with other members of AHC, while knowing that the produce we bring to market goes directly to people who need a fresh local food source.

—VAL STEINBRONN, OWNER, VALLEE GIRL FARMS

Through its recently introduced microloan program, the CFB similarly encourages self-reliance and entrepreneurship among participants in the local food system. This program, developed in partnership with the Community Investment Corporation, offers small, short-term loans to local farmers and startup food businesses whose goals and strategies complement the overall mission of the CFB. In 2107, $10,500 in short-term loans helped three local businesses: Gourmet Cookies by Delma, Bajo Tierra Kitchen, and Pivot Produce, all of which emphasize the use of high-quality, locally sourced ingredients in their products.

With poverty comes not just food insecurity and chronic illness but, often, social isolation. Of course, you don't have to be poor or homebound to suffer from the behavioral effects of loneliness, such as anxiety and depression. Yet loneliness is a fact of life for many seniors living on a fixed income, whether in an urban setting like Tucson, a suburban area such as Marana, or a rural town like Tombstone. Addressing this important yet often neglected issue and, more generally, the well-being of its elderly clients, is now a priority of the CFB.

Charlie, CFB Client, with Daisy

I lost my husband nineteen years ago. Everything was fine at first. But you get older and your bank account dwindles. You're on a fixed income and it's just never enough.

I've been coming to the food bank for about two years. The first time I came I really didn't know what to expect, but everyone was so friendly!

It gives you peace of mind to know there's a place you can always go, that you don't have to just sit at home and be hungry.

The fresh vegetables at the food bank are my favorite. Even my dog Daisy likes them. I'm just grateful for everything we get.

—CHARLIE, CFB CLIENT

To most of us, these crippling problems experienced by the poor seem utterly overwhelming. Is it realistic, then, for a food bank, even one as innovative as the CFB, to think it can actually solve *all* of them?

Probably not. Nevertheless, if food banks are to give their clients realistic hope for a brighter future, it is clearly not enough to simply give them greater access to healthier food, improved social services, or even the educational tools to advocate for themselves.

The bottom line is that the unemployed also need *jobs*, and the underemployed need decent, better-paying ones—the kind that provide a livable wage, sufficient to help raise the quality of their lives, reduce everyday stress, and ultimately provide a sustainable way out of poverty.

This is not exactly news to anyone concerned about the plight of the poor in our country. The importance of providing a livable wage has long been recognized by social activists and progressive thinkers, such as the CFB's founders and its own visionary, Punch Woods.

Although many cities, including Tucson, have now passed living wage initiatives, the fact remains that much more than simply raising the minimum wage needs to be done if we are to achieve economic justice for all.

The CFB, once again, is taking the lead in the community it serves. In 2011, the CFB developed the Caridad Community Kitchen in Tucson. Caridad's signature ten-week Culinary Training Program gives unemployed and underemployed adults the skills needed for careers in the food industry. Caridad's operational capacity was expanded substantially in 2018 with a generous gift from the Kautz Family Foundation that doubled the size of the building; thirty-five students received training in that year.

Caridad Community Kitchen, 2020 (Russell Varineau)

Students at Caridad Community Kitchen

Since the program's inception, 193 students have graduated, and about 85 percent have found employment. As part of their training, students prepare meals that are distributed at various sites in the community and to other groups through Caridad's catering service. They are guided by a staff of fifteen and helped by about 300 volunteers.

The experience of Jesse Segebartt, a Caridad graduate, is typical of those whose lives have been changed dramatically through their participation in this innovative program. Jesse later put his training to work as a valued member of Caridad's staff.

We give to causes we believe in. The CFB does a great job with things that we can't do, and it is needed. Southern Arizona is blessed to have the CFB because it covers such a large area, helps so many people, and is a very important resource.

We especially love the emphasis on providing access to fresh food through the farmers' markets and the garden program. That addition of healthy food makes a big difference in people's lives. We're happy to be a part of that difference.

—JIM AND MARY KAUTZ, CFB DONORS

Jim and Mary Kautz, CFB Donors

In May of 2014, I was accepted into Class 10 of Caridad's Culinary Training Program. As someone with a felony record, work was hard to come by and formal education was far outside of my budget. Caridad offered me the skills necessary to approach employers with confidence—not only in my skillset, but in myself.

In July of that year, I accepted an on-call position, and over time worked my way up to serving the program as Lead Cook of the Culinary Training and Community Meals programs. Students come from many backgrounds, and every class comes with its own personal lessons on cultural, financial and physical barriers.

Ultimately, the class gave me a career. But working with the fifteen classes that have graduated since my own has provided personal validation in my role in actualizing the hefty mission of the CFB as a whole.

—JESSE SEGEBARTT, LEAD COOK, CULINARY TRAINING AND COMMUNITY MEALS PROGRAMS, CARIDAD COMMUNITY KITCHEN

Jesse Segebartt, Lead Cook of Culinary Training and Community Meals, Caridad Community Kitchen

The recent expansion of Caridad's kitchen facilities was designed specifically to help more seniors, one of the CFB's major goals moving forward. Meals are designed to fit their special nutritional needs, and are delivered to them through a partnership with Pima Council on Aging, Catholic Community Services, and Lutheran Social Services of the Southwest. In 2018, 328,000 meals were prepared, a 177 percent increase over the previous year.

Caridad is a model for what the CFB hopes to accomplish in the future by providing its clients with increased access to economic opportunity.

Caridad's Culinary Training Program is a natural fit for an organization centered around food. But are there other kinds of job training programs that the new CFB can develop for its clients—ones that also provide a living wage, and not just a job but a career with the potential for advancement? With its current emphasis on improving clients' long-term health, the CFB, logically, could partner with agencies that offer training for careers in healthcare.

CHAPTER 11

IT TAKES YOU

If you can't feed a hundred people, then feed just one.
−MOTHER THERESA

TO SUPPORT CARIDAD COMMUNITY KITCHEN, Las Milpitas Community Farm, the Gabrielle Giffords Resource Center, and numerous new programs such as the nutrition initiatives for children and seniors—in other words, to advance its ambitious community-development/education agenda—the CFB has amped up fundraising in recent years. The 140 third-party fundraising events that were held in 2016 generated $368,000 and 1.4-million meals for the needy, and 1,257 food drives helped collect almost a million pounds of food, equivalent to about 800,000 meals.

The annual Winterhaven Festival of Lights food drive and the Letter Carriers Stamp Out Hunger® Food Drive continue to be the largest of the CFB's food drives, bringing in about one-third of the roughly 900,000 pounds of food donated in 2019. But new and novel drives are introduced regularly, such as Canstruction®, sponsored by the Society for Design Administration (SDA), in which colossal structures made of food cans are showcased, then distributed to food banks. In 2016, the Canstruction® event collected 10,216 pounds of food.

SDA's Canstruction® Food Drive

Letter Carriers Stamp Out Hunger® Food Drive

HSL's Stuff the Bus Food Drive

Tucson Roadrunners Food Drive

Winterhaven Festival of Lights Food Drive

Sio Castillo, CFB Chief
Development Officer

Our fundraising team works to inspire the public to give back, from holding our annual signature events like HungerWalk to educating our communities about the pervasiveness of hunger today. We are fortunate to work in an extremely generous community where neighbors are always willing to step up to help others. The task of ending hunger is possible only because of our CFB family—our generous donors who are changing lives in southern Arizona.

—SIO CASTILLO, CFB CHIEF DEVELOPMENT OFFICER

TEP Powerful Choice Challenge Donation

Farm to Table Fund-a-Need Auction

Thanksgiving on the Mayflower Event

Without the continued generosity of the CFB's many corporate and individual donors, its diverse programming would not be possible. In 2017, about 29,000 community members donated more than $11 million. This contribution is especially vital today in light of the problems faced by nonprofits like the CFB competing for an ever-dwindling supply of government funds.

For example, in 2017, the CFB received $125,000 from Tucson Electric Power (TEP) as part of the company's Powerful Choice Challenge program. The Walmart Foundation contributed $55,000 in 2018 to support the development of the CFB's seniors-nutrition initiative. These funds will help staff go out into the community to educate and enroll more qualifying seniors in the SNAP program.

The E.W. Scripps Company was another invaluable supporter. For many years, through its 94.9 MIXfm radio affiliate, it hosted the CFB's signature Thanksgiving on the Mayflower annual event, which brought in about a million dollars and 50,000 pounds of food.

Donations by individuals, however, remain the backbone of the CFB's fundraising efforts. Most are relatively small, yet together their impact is enormous. These gifts demonstrate how effectively individuals can contribute as changemakers in a community.

The Farm to Table dinner—one of the CFB's newest fundraisers in support of its healthy food and education initiatives—illustrates the crucial role of individual donors. Guests at this event participate in the Fund-a-Need auction to support a specific program of their choosing, such as the child-nutrition initiative. In the process, they make a real change in someone's life.

It takes the efforts of the CFB's 146 staff members and 6,000 volunteers, working about 200,000 hours annually, to carry out its expanded mission. As in the early days, volunteers are the key. The passion they bring to their work continues unabated. But the scale and complexity of the CFB's operations today demand far more sophisticated methods of training, organizing, and supervising this volunteer workforce.

Each volunteer has a distinctive story to tell, revealing what motivates them. Yet, whether driving a delivery truck or serving as a board member, they all share the same commitment to helping the less fortunate among us.

Toby Schneider, CFB Volunteer

I am a volunteer driver for the CFB. I deliver food to libraries, schools, and the Tucson Urban League. Through the child-nutrition initiative, I deliver fruit, energy bars, snacks, regular milk, chocolate milk, and cereal. When school is out, the libraries act as day-care centers where parents drop off their children when they leave for work. In the summer, I deliver even more food to more libraries for these children.

I love doing this volunteer work because teachers tell me that the children's attention span is much better after they eat breakfast. When I was a child, my father was a minister and we didn't have much money. I had cereal and milk for breakfast every day, and I was hungry before lunch. I remember those days, and I'm thrilled to be able to help provide food for kids in the morning.

—TOBY SCHNEIDER, CFB VOLUNTEER

Nathan Rothschild, CFB Board Member

What motivates me to serve on the CFB board is a desire to serve the community and especially those who are in need of our help the most. Two events from my childhood have inspired me to do this work and support the CFB's new initiatives.

When I was young, I worked with my father in a community garden. From this I learned not only the importance of fresh food but also of self-sufficiency, two priorities of the CFB's education agenda. I also remember the special way my grandfather would look at me when I would eat. He was a Holocaust survivor, and the sheer joy that watching others eat gave him left me with an indelible memory of the power of both food and starvation.

What troubles me daily is that here in the wealthiest country in the world there are so many of our own citizens who lack the resources needed to put healthy food on the table. Healthy food is the basis of healthy living. By serving on the CFB board, I hope to help bring this essential building block to all in our community.

— NATHAN ROTHSCHILD, CFB BOARD MEMBER

Susan Barrable, CFB Board Member and Marana Resource Center
Advisory Board Member

While I now serve on the CFB's board, I started volunteering ten years ago in the warehouse at the Marana Resource Center. Working directly with our clients as I prepacked the carts with nonperishable food was a truly reward-ing yet humbling experience. I witnessed our clients' dignity and their shame; their demands and their acceptance; their comfort and their discomfort; their resilience and their vulnerability. Who wants to have to come to a food bank to receive food, which surely is a basic human right? And it was not lost on me that, given a change in circumstances, it could be any one of us in that food bank line.

It dawned on me, as the months went by, that food banking was big business in America, which seemed immoral. And I often imagined how wonderful it would be if we could put food banks out of business. I now understand how naive I was, and how incredibly complex and intertwined the issues of hunger and poverty are. Yet it is difficult for me to get past the appalling statistics that one-in-six people in this country experience hunger or food insecurity, while we discard more than enough food to meet that real and urgent need for assistance.

—SUSAN BARRABLE, CFB BOARD MEMBER AND MARANA
RESOURCE CENTER ADVISORY BOARD MEMBER

CHAPTER 12

IT TAKES RESEARCH AND THE SHARING OF KNOWLEDGE

Research is creating new knowledge.

—NEIL ARMSTRONG

IF WE ARE TO END hunger in our communities, it will clearly take more than food. Rather than just a handout, a hand *up* is needed. And those we are trying to help need to have a strong voice in the process. We need to listen carefully to what they really want.

But how can we measure progress in ending hunger and breaking the cycle of poverty that is its cause? How can we determine what works and what doesn't? And how can such knowledge be applied on the ground to make food banks more effective agents of change?

Useful answers to these questions are likely to come out of the CFB's recent work bringing together leaders from local and national organizations to share their experiences, best practices, and ideas, all aimed at moving beyond hunger relief and creating a thriving community.

In 2012, for example, the CFB cosponsored the Border Food Summit in Rio Rico, Arizona, and organized, in partnership with the Pima County Food Systems Alliance, the Leap What You Sow Conference, which brought together more than one-hundred farmers and community activists to discuss ways to work more effectively together on local food access and market issues. Then, in 2013, it created and sponsored the first Closing the Hunger Gap conference in Tucson. More than 300 people attended from 170 different organizations around the country.

Closing the Hunger Gap Conference, 2013

Partner Agency Conference, 2018

The success of this conference led to the creation of the Closing the Hunger Gap network, which now organizes bi-annual conferences in other cities. This nationwide network functions as a kind of think tank, addressing these five main strategic priorities:

1. Positioning food banks and food programs as public health institutions
2. Building local food systems and community economies
3. Growing capacity as community organizers and social justice advocates
4. Collaborating for clients: wrap-around services
5. Advocating for policy and funding conditions that support community food security

Not surprisingly, the strategic priorities of the Closing the Hunger Gap network mirror those of the CFB today. In 2016, the CFB also sponsored the first annual Partner Agency Conference, attended by 125 local nonprofits. The information shared among participating agencies will no doubt allow them to serve their clients more effectively and, ideally, help improve the overall quality of client lives in ways that are most meaningful to them.

Equally promising are the CFB's recent efforts advocating for and partnering with local communities to achieve similar goals through research and action plans carried out largely by their own residents. Government-sponsored community development programs, whether abroad in rural areas of developing countries or in our own economically depressed urban neighborhoods, have had, at best, mixed results through the decades. Witness the often-disastrous effects of urban renewal in many of our inner cities, including the misguided destruction in the 1960s of one of downtown Tucson's oldest Mexican-American neighborhoods.

These programs have been criticized for imposing culturally inappropriate policies and economic development strategies on low-income neighborhoods in the name of "progress,"

La Doce Barrio Foodways Project Report, 2018 (La Doce Barrio Foodways Project)

Citizen Ethnographers, La Doce Barrio Foodways Project, 2017 (La Doce Barrio Foodways Project)

while not paying enough attention to residents' shared history, values, and customs. For too long, the self-interests of government bureaucrats and commercial developers have shaped the lives of the poor. For too long, their voices have been ignored.

La Doce Barrio Foodways Project is now attempting to rectify this problem. This project was sponsored in 2017 by the CFB in partnership with the City of Tucson, the Southwest Folklife Alliance, the Community Foundation of Southern Arizona, and Tierra Y Libertad Organization.

La Doce is an historic Tucson neighborhood stretching for three miles along South Twelfth Avenue. Focusing on food but encompassing other aspects of this community's Hispanic heritage and distinctive culture, the innovative project based in the neighborhood used twenty local high school students as "citizen ethnographers" to gather data about their specific needs and wishes from 228 residents and visitors.

Project organizers made the decision to invest the majority of the grant funds in support of grassroot leadership, which included stipends for the student researchers and the community elders. Nelda Ruiz, a community organizer and neighborhood resident, was hired as Project Manager. She worked in close collaboration with Dr. Rebecca Crocker, an ethnographer affiliated with the Southwest Folklife Alliance and the University of Arizona, as well as with Nick Henry, former CFB Director of Resource Centers and Health Initiatives.

The findings, published in a 2018 report and presented in the documentary film *La Doce Barrio Foodways*, chart a course of action aimed at exercising local control over economic development and residents' well-being, consistent with their cultural priorities. La Doce Barrio Foodways Project promises to be a model for the future development of similar urban communities in Tucson, as well as those in the wider rural region the CFB serves.

Dr. Rebecca Crocker (*left*), Lead Ethnographer, and Nelda Ruiz (*right*), Project Manager, La Doce Barrio Foodways Project

La Doce Barrio Foodways Project turned a lot of common wisdom on its head. It showed that ethnographic expertise should not be the exclusive domain of academics and other highly trained individuals, but rather is most powerful when placed into the hands of engaged community members eager to see their community through new eyes.

Our findings moved beyond the scope of food into well-being, health, cultural heritage, and social transformation. Our team of citizen ethnographers found that food acts as a social glue and a means of cultural continuity and health maintenance. We mapped native plants and edible fruits growing in barrio gardens and tasted cherished family recipes. We talked to residents about their desire to participate in their communities; their disconnection from city government; and their visions for common gathering spaces, more fresh foods, and safer streets. Our report highlights recommendations for resident-driven change in South Tucson, such as alternative models of local governance and community land trusts.

The CFB's participation was invaluable; they offered their staff time to manage this project and keep us on track, facilitate meetings, and build connections based on their wealth of social capital with other organizations and governmental agencies. Their dedication to this project is testament to their commitment to building local leadership, supporting grassroots activism, and raising up the voices of smaller organizations and underrepresented populations.

—DR. REBECCA CROCKER, LEAD ETHNOGRAPHER,
LA DOCE BARRIO FOODWAYS PROJECT

Nick Henry, Former CFB
Director of Resource Centers
and Health Initiatives

Our work with La Doce Barrio Foodways Project is a shift in our way of thinking at the CFB. We know that we can't do it all, and we know that we don't have all the answers. The people in the communities we serve understand the problems they are facing all too well, and they are capable of building a vision and working towards a better future. At the CFB, we are at our best when we are serving as a partner to the community in this effort—helping give voice to their vision, connecting them to resources, and making it happen.

During La Doce project, I met with community partners and on-the-ground organizers every two weeks for over a year. It was refreshing and inspiring getting to sit at the table with these amazing folks, and being a peer and partner to them as their vision took hold and began to grow. We are excited to move on to the next phase!

—NICK HENRY, FORMER CFB DIRECTOR OF
RESOURCE CENTERS AND HEALTH INITIATIVES

The CFB's commitment to research as a means to improve client services is clearly evident in its collaborative work with the University of Arizona's Bureau of Applied Research in Anthropology (BARA). BARA staff and interns, for example, have developed client satisfaction surveys to help the CFB assess the effectiveness of its programs and introduce change where needed.

As BARA's work suggests, the University of Arizona has contributed greatly to the CFB's success as an agent of change in the community. The CFB–University of Arizona joint Food Safari Nutrition Education Program was mentioned previously and, through the years, the two institutions have partnered in many projects. The CFB has collaborated with the university's Frances McClelland Institute for Children, Youth, and Families; the Agnese Nelms Haury Program in Environment and Social Justice, and the Eller College of Management Social Innovation programs.

Dr. Diane Austin, Director of BARA,
University of Arizona

The CFB's dedication to evidence-based program development and evaluation of its impact is clearly evident in its ongoing collaborative work with the Bureau of Applied Research in Anthropology (BARA), a research unit housed in the University of Arizona's School of Anthropology. BARA's first project for the CFB, in 2003, was an exploration of the potential for expanding the use of SNAP benefits at local farmers' markets. However, interactions between the two organizations were sporadic until 2012, when the CFB became one of the core community partners in BARA's internship program.

Three areas of focus are: client satisfaction surveys that help the organization assess its Emergency Food Assistance Program; needs and assets assessments in neighborhoods and communities within the CFB service area; and food production and community building at Las Milpitas Community Farm. BARA researchers also have collaborated with the CFB to understand opportunities and challenges associated with the organization's move to understand and address food and social justice.

—DR. DIANE AUSTIN, DIRECTOR OF BARA,
UNIVERSITY OF ARIZONA

Compost Cats is another innovative collaboration. This student-led program provides training and demonstrations in state-of-the-art composting techniques, aimed at diverting waste in Tucson and other southern Arizona communities, while giving the CFB access to a nutrient-rich soil amendment for its community gardens.

One of the most promising recent partnerships focuses on research into diet-related disease. The aim of this research, conducted by the University of Arizona's Department of Nutritional Sciences and the College of Public Health, is to improve the health of the CFB's clients.

Compost Cats at Work

Dr. Douglas Taren, Professor and
Associate Dean, Mel and Enid
Zuckerman College of Public Health

As a public health nutritionist and researcher, I have been very impressed with how the CFB does research before starting new programs or changing existing programs, all aimed at improving their services and the health of their clients. In these studies, the CFB has collaborated with the University of Arizona's Department of Nutritional Sciences and its Mel and Enid Zuckerman College of Public Health to get a better understanding of how the food that is distributed affects the diet of their clients, and also to ensure that it meets their dietary needs, especially those with chronic diseases such as diabetes.

The CFB is constantly working with new partners to test new delivery systems for their programs. For example, their current USDA-funded research program is testing out how to distribute prescription food boxes by working with two federally funded community health centers that have clinics in Cochise County, Arizona, and El Rio Health, which has clinics in Tucson. These evidence-based approaches are national models for food banks.

—DR. DOUGLAS TAREN, PROFESSOR
AND ASSOCIATE DEAN, MEL AND ENID
ZUCKERMAN COLLEGE OF PUBLIC HEALTH,
UNIVERSITY OF ARIZONA

Feeding America, the national network of food banks, has in the past come under some criticism for overemphasizing hunger relief and charity and not doing enough to shorten the food line. But that is changing as the network now puts its resources to work initiating research programs that address the root causes of hunger and that provide solutions to the related health problems of the working poor, minority groups, and the most vulnerable populations: children and seniors. For example, Feeding America is sponsoring research on the critical relationship between income, diet, and health, including a landmark study on the disproportionate incidence of diabetes among the poor and the ways food banks can help those suffering from this and other chronic diseases.

As this research is put into practice and other food banks begin to follow the example of the CFB as a changemaker, there is indeed reason to believe that significant progress will be made in the fight against hunger and poverty.

Research demonstrates that people experiencing food insecurity are at higher risk for poor health, especially nutrition-related chronic diseases like hypertension and diabetes. Feeding America and member food banks have increasingly focused efforts to better understand and address the intersections between food insecurity and health.

Over the last decade, we have collectively conducted several studies on how food banks can provide support to people living with prediabetes and diabetes; developed resources to advance food bank–health care partnerships; and implemented new programming models to improve nutrition, food security, and health within the communities we serve. For example, one focus area has been on providing medically-tailored food packages to adults living with diabetes. Findings from a pilot study and follow-up randomized trial demonstrate that food banks can improve dietary intake and support clients' capacities for diabetes self-management.

We believe collaborating with food banks, agency partners, and healthcare and other organizations is critical in order to successfully address the links between hunger and health. We also believe this work is essential for promoting wellness and advancing health equity in the United States.

—MORGAN SMITH, SENIOR MANAGER,
HEALTH & NUTRITION, FEEDING AMERICA

CHAPTER 13

A FUTURE WITHOUT HUNGER?

The day hunger is eradicated from the earth there will be the greatest spiritual explosion the world has ever seen.

-FEDERICO GARCÍA LORCA

MORE THAN FORTY YEARS AGO, the founders of the CFB envisioned a hunger-free community and a time when food banks would be obsolete. While this dream has not yet been realized, it is still alive today, evident in the tireless efforts of the CFB's dedicated staff and volunteers and in their plans for the future.

As the history of the CFB demonstrates, meaningful progress in the battle against hunger has been made. Indeed, we are today moving from feeding the food line to shortening it. But can we ever truly eliminate it?

The cynical will argue that the goal of ending hunger is a pipe dream, one impossible to achieve in America unless our capitalist system, which at its core perpetuates economic inequality, is radically altered. Although there is some truth to this claim, there is more in the belief shared by most of us that helping the needy is the most important thing we can do.

If we were to look ahead to a time and place where there is no hunger, we would notice a different social consciousness. There would be an underlying assumption that just as everyone has the right to breathe clean air, drink clean water, so would everyone have the right to enough to eat.

—PUNCH WOODS, "PUNCHLINE," MARCH/APRIL 1990

My desired future is that we will raise the issue of hunger as a critical matter for our nation's attention. In this scenario, as agents of change, we would open questions about why hunger continues to exist in a nation with such wealth, so much talent, and so much caring. We must not only raise the issue intentionally, consistently, and effectively, but organize efforts to address it, including through public advocacy.

Some might question if this might erode some of the financial support food banks are receiving from those who benefit from the status quo. This may happen, and food bank boards will then have to consider how to address it, or succumb to the easy answer of being willing to have their silence bought.

— MARK HOMAN, CFB COFOUNDER

At middle age, the CFB is at the top of its game in being the go-to hunger-relief charity in southern Arizona, and is poised to either breathe life into the capacity of the next generation of mission advocates and community leaders, or fall into myopia and obsolescence.

While the CFB still has much to do to scale its own—and its agency partners'—capacity to acquire, store, and distribute the amount and variety of healthy food needed in persistently impoverished southern Arizona for all families to flourish nutritionally, economically, and socially, the next stage of life for CFB will be to more effectively scale our work to end hunger at its root causes in poverty.

And this goes beyond merely connecting neighbors in need to food or other vital socioeconomic resources. It means connecting neighbors to neighbors—the grassroots to the grass-middles to the grass-tops—if we're to have productive and equitable relations among diverse people across diverse communities, and commonsensically solve problems together for our common good.

—MICHAEL MCDONALD, CFB CEO

While food bankers often say they work to 'end hunger,' the reality is food banking alone is not capable of ending hunger in the United States. My experience proved to me that food banks provide only about 15 percent of the emergency and supplemental food needed to sustain hungry Americans. Can hungry people be expected to exist on merely 15 percent of three meals a day, 365 days a year? I think that is ludicrous, but we also have not come to a collective philosophy that food is a basic human right.

In the United States, we lack the essential national element of a robust 'food and nutrition policy.' We have settled for programs (federal, local, and faith-based) to fill gaps, but we have no specific policy that provides a mandate for those programs to exist. Therefore, they are treated as discretionary and are easily cut or eliminated when congressional and other budgets are tight.

If we are truly serious about being 'hunger-free' in our country, we must address the larger issues creating hunger, such as income inequality, low wages, lack of affordable housing, health care, childcare, transportation, the growing number of seniors on fixed incomes, and equitable access to healthy, affordable, and culturally appropriate food.

We've made progress, but there is still much difficult and life-changing work to be done.

—GINNY HILDEBRAND, FORMER DIRECTOR OF
THE ASSOCIATION OF ARIZONA FOOD BANKS

Food banks are amazing organizations filled with talented people who contribute to their communities and regions in so many positive ways. Our members are getting better, more effective, and more efficient at sourcing nutritious food that would otherwise go to waste and distributing it to people facing hunger. In addition, food banks are working with farmers and retailers to capture more nutritious food, teaching people about the importance of good nutrition, advocating on behalf of the people they serve, and collaborating with other community organizations to provide integrated solutions that improve lives.

Yes, food banks are leaders in distributing much-needed food, but they are also leading the effort to improve society. This evolution will continue in the years to come until we end hunger in America.

—MATT KNOTT, FORMER PRESIDENT OF FEEDING AMERICA

I am now resigned to the fact that food banks are necessary and not going out of business any time soon. And so, I take solace in the fact that the CFB does so much more than provide food.

We reduce waste by capturing fresh food and produce that would otherwise go into the landfill, whilst redirecting it to people who need it. We provide other resources to, and work with, those in need, in an effort to help break the cycle of poverty. We continue to work with our partners to strengthen and help communities to become more self-sufficient. And for many we are often simply a lifeline for those who may have given up hope, and find themselves in the undignified position of lining up at a food bank to access a basic necessity.

The ongoing challenge continues to be enormous and quite overwhelming. I consider it my duty to continue to serve the community to the best of my ability—with compassion, dignity and nonjudgement for those we serve—and trust that somewhere along the line, I am able to make a small difference in some people's lives. After all, nobody chooses to go hungry.

—SUSAN BARRABLE, CFB BOARD MEMBER AND MARANA RESOURCE
CENTER ADVISORY BOARD MEMBER

POSTSCRIPT

THE CFB'S RESPONSE TO THE COVID-19 PANDEMIC

DECEMBER 2020

IN SPRING 2020, THE COVID-19 virus hit while this book was being prepared for publication. The pandemic's effect on low-income people—especially those of color—has been devastating. The World Bank projects that about 100 million people will fall back into extreme poverty this year. Feeding America estimates that, in the United States, the number of people experiencing food insecurity will increase from about thirty-five million to as many as fifty-four million.

With unemployment in southern Arizona approaching record levels, the number of its food-insecure residents rose proportionately. Many of them, including the most vulnerable seniors, had never before used the services of a food bank. According to Feeding America, in the early days of the pandemic, four in ten food bank users were first-timers.

During the first months of the pandemic, the CFB distributed about 22 percent more food boxes than in the same period in 2019. The spike was even greater in rural service areas: about 30 percent higher in, for example, Graham and Greenlee counties. An Associated Press analysis of data from 181 food banks in the Feeding America network suggests that this dire situation appears to have worsened throughout the United States during the autumn spike of COVID-19: In the third quarter of 2020, almost 60 percent more people received emergency food boxes than in the third quarter of 2019.

The sudden, dramatic rise in the demand for the CFB's hunger-relief services put an unprecedented amount of pressure on the organization's resources and personnel. Moreover, the highly contagious nature of the virus presented unique challenges for safe food distribution. The CFB had to adapt and, once again, reinvent itself.

In March 2020, to meet the increased demand as well as lessen the risk of spreading the virus among staff, volunteers, and clients, the CFB initiated several vital operational changes. Food distribution at most of its main pantries—the resource centers in Tucson, Marana, and Green Valley—was temporarily suspended. A food distribution *drive-through* model was adopted. In Tucson, the large parking lots at the Kino Sports Complex were used for this purpose. The work of assembling food boxes and directing the drive-through distribution was carried out largely by members of the National Guard, assisted by CFB staff reassigned to the front line of the hunger-relief effort. A similar drive-through model was used at the CFB's Santa Cruz River Farmers' Market.

Consistent with the goal of reducing risk, the use of volunteers—many of them high-risk seniors—was severely limited. CFB employees, along with Pima County staff, were redeployed to replace them at various sites and carry out their traditional warehouse work at the Punch Woods Multi-Service Center, as well as prepare senior meals and distribute grab-and-go food packages at the Caridad Community Kitchen. At the Nogales Resource Center, the National Guard and Wilson Produce also assisted the CFB in the shipping of produce to partner agencies in Pima and Cochise counties.

As a result of the pandemic, the CFB expanded its community partnerships throughout southern Arizona. This work was essential in maintaining the health of low-income families. Fresh produce was distributed to schools in the Tucson Unified, Amphi Unified,

Volunteer Distributing Food at Kino Sports Complex During Pandemic, 2020

Line of Cars at Kino Sports Complex During Pandemic, 2020

Drive-Through Santa Cruz River Farmers' Market During Pandemic, 2020

Sunnyside Unified, and Safford Unified school districts. Branches of the Pima County Public Library also received produce to be distributed to children in their BackPacks. The CFB enabled eleven emergency feeding organizations in Pima and Cochise counties to distribute hot meals to high-need populations, including children, tribal members, and the homebound.

Looking ahead, one of the biggest challenges will be making up for the shortfall in resources due to the cancellation of the CFB's annual food drives. Most food had to be purchased, the funds derived in part from government grants. The annual HungerWalk fundraising event became a virtual one in 2020.

Despite all these obstacles and disruptions, the CFB continued to invest substantially in the community. In 2020, it granted more than $1.5 million to nonprofits, tribal groups, resource centers, and aid organizations to further its mission, emphasizing not only hunger relief but education, advocacy, and social justice.

And one program has remained fully operational throughout the pandemic: Las Milpitas Community Farm. In fact, it has been thriving, with community participation at an all-time high. For the first time, all of the farm's garden plots are in use, and there is even a waiting list for new families. Las Milpitas increased seed distribution and launched more virtual live trainings and educational videos.

The CFB's response to the pandemic has been extraordinarily effective, yet perhaps not entirely unexpected; over the course of its long history, the CFB has demonstrated time and time again that it can find and implement creative ways to help the needy. Its egalitarian tradition of caring, sharing, and innovating remains vibrant.

ACKNOWLEDGMENTS

THIS BOOK IS THE END product of the CFB's History Project, and would not have been possible without the generous assistance of many of its former and current staff members and volunteers.

I would like to thank Dan Duncan, Mark Homan, Ginny Hildebrand, Joy Tucker, and Varga Garland for their invaluable insights into the early history of the CFB and food banking in Arizona and the United States. Michael McDonald, Robert Ojeda, Dana Yost, and Brandi Smith provided comprehensive data about the CFB's current mission and operations. Discussions with Christina Whitworth and Gary Nusinov helped shape the book's content and design. Amy Cross, Haley Knapp, Dan Singleton, Katherine Zuniga-Loncharich, Susan Barrable, and Sio Castillo kindly provided their editorial, production, and marketing expertise. Russell Varineau provided technical assistance in the field. Varga Garland, Dr. Ron Sparks, Alex Laetsch, Bruce Hilpert, and Diane Dittemore critiqued early drafts of the book, and their suggestions are greatly appreciated.

I am grateful to the following staff members of the University of Arizona Press for recognizing the book's potential and guiding its design, production, and marketing: Kathryn Conrad, Director; Kristen Buckles, Editor-In-Chief; Amanda Kraus, Editorial, Design, and Production Manager; Leigh McDonald, Art Director and Book Designer; Abby Mogollón, Marketing Manager. I thank freelancer Edie Jarolim for her excellent copyediting of the final manuscript.

Two individuals deserve special mention for their contributions. The late Charles "Punch" Woods provided his distinctive perspective on the CFB's evolution. In several interviews, Punch shed light on the people, events, and forces shaping the CFB's success, as well as on the bigger picture of food banking set against the plight of the food insecure in the last quarter of the twentieth century.

Kristen Quinnan, the CFB's former Director of Community Engagement, made essential contributions during the research and manuscript-development phases. Along with offering enthusiastic moral support consistently over the course of several years, she helped me navigate the CFB's archives, select photos, and coordinate site visits and interviews with CFB participants. Her role in this project's success cannot be overstated.

INDEX

Page numbers in *italics* refer to photographs or illustrations.

ABOUT THE AUTHOR

Dr. Seth Schindler is an anthropologist and former Curator of Ethnological Collections at the Arizona State Museum. He has served as an NEH Research Fellow and Weatherhead Resident Scholar at the School for Advanced Research. Dr. Schindler's specialties are diverse, ranging from the tribal art of New Guinea to the material culture of the Seri Indians of Sonora, Mexico, and the cultural history of the Southwest. He has contributed articles to academic journals such as *American Anthropologist*, and to books for the general public, including *The Encyclopedia of Anthropology*.